DATA DRIVEN DEALINGS DEVELOPMENT

Analyzing, Predicting, and Recommending
Sales Items per Customer using
Python Machine Learning Models

Jesko Rehberg

If Cash is King,

Cash Flow is Queen,

and Profit is Prince,

..then Data is Ace!

Thanks to my family and friends,

without them this work would not make any sense.

Cover Picture:

Inspired by flowers we will visualize our sales item connections and clusters via Network Graph..

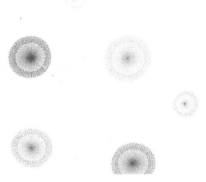

.. knowing that we will not even come close to the beauty of nature!

CONTENTS

AIM

When starting my data analysis journey, I needed books or tutorials covering all the topics involved to run a sales analysis in Python successfully. Especially when you are a complete newbie, analyzing A-Z without any (or insufficient) pre-knowledge is difficult because most books only cover specific parts of the whole project, and it is challenging to put all the puzzle pieces together. That is my primary motivation for writing this book: you to have one guideline in hand that leads through your whole sales analysis project, from installing all the necessary Python libraries, cleaning the data, effectively training the Machine Learning (ML) models, and deploying the results to your colleagues in an intelligible way.

For this reason this book is divided into two main chapters:

1. General Setup and necessary common basic understanding
 In this chapter, we will learn how to install Python, become familiar with pip installing libraries (libraries that make our life so much easier and which make Python such an excellent coding language), know how to fork other people's code projects from Github, get in contact with our new friends from Stackoverflow and Kaggle and becoming a cloud-native (okay, at least becoming familiar with the related cloud aspects for this project).

We will also compile an overview of the most essential notations (and that is not only because many of them sound so hip) when it comes to talking about and understanding ML.

This knowledge is an essential basic premise when dealing with ML algorithms to ensure we do not get washed away by the overwhelming ML/Artificial Intelligence (AI)/Data Science (DS) waves.

2. Analysis

Now that we have all the tools, we will move to our main aim: deep analysis of our customers' market baskets/ sales data. I will explain all the code blocks to make them easily digestible. All the code details and necessary theoretical background are described here in this chapter, so you do not need to switch back to Chapter 1 to understand the code. In contrast to Chapter 1, Chapter 2 is the pragmatic coding part, and with all the background, we will need to understand what, why, and how we are coding. Chapter 1 is more about the overall technical setup and general concepts. We will execute all analyses in Chapter 2 using Jupyter Notebook on Colab. You can also run this Jupyter Notebook on your local machine. You will find all necessary modifications commented on in the code. We will discuss how to showcase the results to our colleagues, also called storytelling or offering a data product. And we certainly want to do that because what`s the use of conducting statistics if we are not understandably sharing our results?

You will find all of my books written this way. So, if you should already be familiar with Chapter 1, you can skip it and jump directly into the coding part in Chapter 2.

By the way, even if it sounded a little unrealistic, there are more things to life than coding Python trying to predict future sales. Please consider your (social) health and take breaks between your coding sessions. For instance, maybe you want to turn your PC off and go out tonight to be inspired by the art that surrounds you:

Böhler & Orendt, Die Verhältnisse, 2011, wooden objects on wall boards, 210 × 440 × 25 cm

Sometimes, this will even give you an unforeseeable fresh perspective on your current project. Just take your share of the pie; it's all out there waiting for you!

AUDIENCE

I wrote this book with people in mind who want to run an analysis on sales data, try to predict future sales, analyze market baskets, and set up a recommending system in Python using statistics and ML frameworks. This step-by-step guideline covers all related topics, so even a beginner without any Python pre-knowledge will be able to complete this job. Every explanation, definition and overall classification is strongly related to our task of analyzing our sales data. This book aims to catch up on all the details we need to understand to predict and recommend sales items. Indeed, there is much more to ML than just predicting sales (e.g., image classification, speech recognition, etc), but that is out of this book`s scope. This book does not focus too much on mathematical or technical backgrounds. Still, more on the pragmatic approach: we will set up a data analysis project from scratch, using a data set that hopefully makes it easy to fit your data. I will explain the code broadly to make it as simple as possible and amend it to your (business) needs. My goal is for you to become a prosperous Python sales forecaster in the shortest time and with no pre-knowledge necessary.

You can find all the code and files necessary for this analysis on my website:

https://Datenanalyse-Rehberg.de

Or my Github account:

https://github.com/DAR-DatenanalyseRehberg.

If you have any questions or feedback about this book, please let me know:

contact@DAR-Analytics.de

ACKNOWLEDGEMENT

Even though this book aims to give you a complete and hands-on guideline, of course, this does not mean you shouldn't read any other books about Python in general or, e.g., predicting sales or recommending systems in particular. With this book, I am trying to put you in a position to reach the finish line in the fast lane. My comments on background are as detailed as we need them to be for us to be successful. But certainly, we can (and should) read much more than only this book since broadening one's mind is never stupid. If you allow me to give you my personalized recommendation, these are the books/resources I find extremely helpful (I do not get any provision for this; I just honestly find these books helpful and very well written):

- All O`Reilly books about Python and "Recommending Systems" in particular.
- The Master Algorithm: How the quest for the utimate learning machine will remake our world, by Pedro Domingos.
  China's President Xi Jinping has this book on his bookshelf, so should we.
- Data Science for Supply Chain Forecast, by Nicolas Vandeput.
  I appreciate Nicolas's evident and easy-to-understand style. Nicolas` approach was so inspiring to me that I took over his idea of looping through the time series data points to predict future sales (see chapter 2.3 in the Jupyter Notebook)
- Moorissa Tjokro

Moorissa is a formidable Data Scientist who shares a lot of gorgeous Jupyter Notebooks. Without her, the Turicreate recommender (see chapter 2.5.6) in this book would not exist:

https://github.com/moorissa

- Mike Bostock

Mike is the inventor of D3 (Data-driven documents javascript) and an outstanding storyteller. Take a look at his work for the New York Times if you are searching for terrific visualization inspiration: https://www.nytimes.com/by/mike-bostock

If you are more of a chatterbox kind of person, there are dozens of great Twitter accounts out there (which are much greater than my @DAR_Analytics, if you allow me this shameless self-promotion):

- @fchollet: creator of Keras, neural networks library.
- @goodfellow: the inventor of GANs and lead author   of deeplearningbook.org
- @JeffDean: Google AI Research and Health
- @kdnuggets: founded by Gregory Piatetsky-Shapiro, including topics like AI, ML, DS, DL, Analytics, Big Data and Data Mining

Although it is unnecessary to understand how to run EDA (Exploratory Data Analysis), predict, and recommend sales items, I think a little bit of pledging allegiance to our coding language, Python, is worth investing time in. Guido van Rossum is the man we owe our coding language, Python:

https://en.wikipedia.org/wiki/Guido_van_Rossum.   Guido invented it, the community built up on it, and you- since latest now with this book in hands - will become a new member of the steadily growing Python community.

By the way, some chapters include a zen of Python in the header.

DATA DRIVEN DEALINGS DEVELOPMENT

I do not take them too seriously, but some are funny and true. We can find the complete list of Python Zen here:

https://www.python.org/dev/peps/pep-0020/

As a last note, I would like to highlight the importance of employees catching up with the knowledge we will have acquired after we have completed this book`s code:

"US faces shortage of 140.000 to 190.000 people with deep analytical skills, as well as 1.5 million managers and analysts with the know-how to use the analysis of big data to make effective decisions" (Mckinsey Global Institute, May 1, 2011 Report).

Deep analytical skills are highly sought-after capabilities not only in the US. This outlook will let you work through the whole project with solid motivation. I am confident our efforts will pay off, and I am honored that you let me join you on your sales analysis path. In the long run, there is no such thing as a finish line regarding our aim to analyze sales data. Still, it is a –with regards to algorithms and frameworks- constantly improving, ongoing, exciting journey.

1. BASIC KNOWLEDGE AND PREREQUISITES

Don't give it to him. He doesn't know what he's doing! (My Aussie tuna fishing boat skipper about me)

Before we start coding, we need to robustly understand the many different techniques and tools we will have under our wings. There is such an overwhelming amount of other algorithms, APIs, approaches, wordings, etc., out there in the world of Python Data Analysis (which some interchangeably would call Data Science, Artificial Intelligence, Predictive Analytics, etc.; see Chapter 1.3) that it can be pretty intimidating for beginners (and not only for them) to get a foot in the door. To ensure we are starting safely, in Chapter 1, we go through all the essential parts we need to understand or set up before conducting the sales analysis, which this book is about. If you are already familiar with specific chapters, you can skip them and proceed with the ones that interest you.

1.1 ANALYSIS OVERVIEW

Now is better than never (Zen of Python)

The pragmatic coding aspects and results (chapter 2) are far more important to us than the theoretical comparison/ classification/distinction of the different techniques, which you hopefully agree with. That is why I will keep this defining chapter 1 as short and straightforward as possible. But you probably already have heard a lot about the often interchangeably used expressions like Machine Learning (ML), Deep Learning (DL), Artificial Intelligence (AI), Data Science (DS), Analytics, Business Intelligence (BI), Data Mining, Data Engineering, Data Warehouse (DWH), Statistical Process Control (SPC), etc. And even though pragmatism stands above theory in this book about sales analysis, we need to have a basic understanding of all these- very often very similar but different- tools and approaches first to make sure that we run our sales analysis in a correct –not misleading- way later on in chapter 2.

Our sales analysis task will guide us the way regarding our necessary theoretical background:

we will have a detailed look at sales data (items sold in quantity/value to customers per day) from the past and analyze it exploratory (EDA, Exploratory Data Analysis, chapter 1.2.2), then we will try to predict the future sales amount as a continuous target given a d-dimension vector (regression, chapter 2.3), use linear algebra for market basket analysis (chapter 2.4), and finally recommend items to our customers (chapter 2.5). One expression that is also very frequently used interchangeably with statistics is the words **analytics** and **analysis.** While the word analysis (discovery, interpretation, and communication of meaningful patterns in data) is apparent to most of us, let us see Wikipedia's definition of analytics: "...Analytics is the systemic computational analysis of data or statistics." Systemic is mainly pointing at the scale here, as data analytics is a broader term for which data analysis is a subcomponent. Data analytics is a superior discipline that embraces the complete management of data. So, Analytics puts even data collection, organization, and storage -including all the tools and techniques used- on top of analysis.

The analysis mainly consists of calculations on our data itself. Data analysis refers to examining, massaging, and arranging a given data set in specific ways to study its parts and support effective decision-making. We will be doing analysis (and not analytics) during chapter 2 because we will not touch the questions about data management in detail. Do you have access directly to ERP Systems, a data warehouse, Access databases, or files? Also, I need to learn your company's principles about data governance. Therefore, we will focus most of our efforts on the analysis and give only a short outlook in places where this makes sense.

Having stated the difference, let us look at an exciting estimation from Aaron Kimball (Wibidata), which I completely agree with: "80% of analytics is sums and averages". I believe that this is (sadly) so true. The media is full of exciting articles about ML/AI. Still, mostly, people are not even adding a standard deviation as a second metric to their mean, which is painful since we have all these great ML techniques accessible, but in real life, too often, people even confuse the difference between mean and median. Another example of how big the gap between the wish for AI/ML and reality is: when was the last time you were confronted with a box plot in your company? At least I have experienced that even though a box plot is a fundamental visualization in descriptive statistics, this handy graph is hardly used or understood in many companies. And how can you know ML if you do not even understand a simple box plot? Of course, we want to do better than that, and shortly, we will attain one of the most exciting parts of this book, namely ML. However, to understand how ML works, we must first understand the main concepts of algebra and its statistics. Even though there is not always a clear separating line- but relatively smooth transitions from one field to the other- understanding the basic concepts behind it will settle the basis for fruitful development in the future. We will discover the statistical concepts pragmatically in detail during our coding part in chapter 2.

1.1.1 LINEAR ALGEBRA AND STATISTICS

Most of us can't wait to get to the ML part, but please hold on young guns. Before discovering the world of these newer concepts, let us first talk about **linear algebra** and **statistics:**

What are the differences between lists, arrays, and vectors? What is meant by sparse matrix and normalization? Why can we sometimes conduct calculations on our data in a plain tabular format, while in other cases, we need to, e.g., unstack the data first (see chapter 2.4)? How can we calculate item-item similarity for recommendations? All we need to understand right now is that the specific algorithm we will use for our analysis dictates the data's desired structure. We will understand what that means in chapter 2, and as soon as we work with vectors, it will lose its horror (I promise we will gain all the necessary knowledge about these concepts during our coding session).

With basic statistics, discussing the theory in more detail before starting to code makes sense. Basic statistics are used when undertaking descriptive statistics like average, median, min, max, range, standard deviation, percentiles, etc., and when building **statistical models**. As an easy example, let us assume we sold a product with a quantity of 5,7,4,8 and 7, as per each sales transaction. The mean (average) quantity for all transactions is the total sum divided by N, so 6.2. And the median would be 4. Mean and median are both estimates (instead called metrics in ML) of **location** (the central tendency of the data, where most of the data is located). What happens if we change the first quantity of 5 into something huge in this number sequence, let's say 19? Our **median** did not change (still 4), but our **mean** changed significantly. The median (50th percentile/quantile, which is technically a weighted average) is a robust metric for data dispersion because it is not sensitive to outliers. At the same time, the mean is not robust against extreme values. Also, the **standard deviation** (as a measure of the mean-variance around the expected data point) increased. Standard deviation is one example of an estimate of **variability**. It measures whether the data values are tightly clustered or spread out. The standard deviation is on the same scale as the original data, making it easier to interpret than pure variance. Variance is the sum of squared deviations from the mean divided by several data values – 1 (see mean squared error, chapter 1.2.5). Standard deviation is the square root of the variance. We are going to use standard deviation in the form of **Euclidean** and **variance for mean squared error** for measuring similarity regarding our recommendings (chapter 2.5.2). The difference between the mean and median is that the median is not influenced by outliers as strongly as the mean. This is the absolute minimum understanding we need to have when discussing the distribution of our data and whether or not outliers (or extraordinary data points) shall be excluded before setting up our model. Using statistics like **histograms, box plots**, **distribution curves**, etc., we can uncover wrongly entered data, which must be corrected or deleted before feeding into our model. Spotting outliers and deciding whether or not the model should include them is one of the most important aspects before setting up a model, whether it is a statistical or an ML model.

Another subfield of statistics is **Statistical Process Control**

(SPC). This is hardly ever mentioned in any ML, AI, or DS books. However, SPC needs to be considered in this analytical concept since it can be helpful in our EDA (chapter 2.1). SPC checks if our processes run stable and closely examines their data distribution. Calculating the 25th (Q2) and 75th (Q3) percentiles (we already talked about the 50th percentile, which is the median), we see the middle 50% of our data. This box plot metric, known as the Interquartile Range (IQR= Q3-Q1), is handy for the first glance at the data's distribution. Furthermore, we can calculate upper and lower control limits in SPC by looking at the data's distribution and calculating the mean and standard deviation (e.g., three times standard deviation when normally distributed; look also for the Six Sigma approach if this should interest you).

This will give us an early indication as soon as the process runs out of **random noise**. I will not explain SPC any further, but in chapter 2.1, we will examine our sales data location and variability very closely.

Descriptive statistics describe our data, but what are **statistical models** used for?

Imagine our sales amount in the past for a specific time frame. It looks like the black dots in the screenshot below. X axis is the time frame, and the y axis represents the sales amount (in other words, data points sales over time):

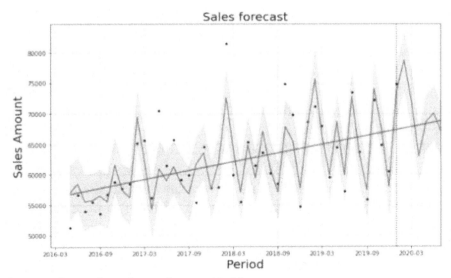

(screenshot taken from chapter 2.3)

If we want to find a function that describes this data (the actual black dots), we have to set up a **model:**

Date is our **independent** variable while sales are **dependent** on it. We can use a linear regression model to describe this data (at least as an overall trend). This well-known statistical model can easily be set up using a tool like Microsoft Excel. Our model for **linear regression** is:

y= m*x+b

and is plotted as the red regression line in the above screenshot (we will explain the blue line and blue shaded area in more detail later in chapter 2).

As we can see, a statistical model formalizes relationships between variables in the data as mathematical equations. It's nothing new, but in case our data points can be described using a linear regression, that's already it. This function puts a straight line through all our data points from the past (sales amount over time), which has the lowest overall deviation with regard to our actual values and the estimated values plotted by this line (see also chapter 1.2.4). Linear regression assumes that there is a linear relationship between the Sales Amount (y) and the time sequence (x). By capturing our data's relationship in a linear regression model, we are able to do two important things. First, we are now able to understand how data affects sales. Second, we are able to fill in the gaps in the dataset to predict future sales. This model could be more precise since many actual values are far from our fitted line. So, the line does not describe our actual data too precisely. This is because our data is not evenly distributed (nothing close to Gaussian with only **random noise** added, and therefore not well to describe via linear regression). It is very unlikely that any real-life sales data has such a simple linear relationship, so performing linear regression will undoubtedly result in some **bias** (see chapter 1.2.5).

That little bit of mathematical function already is our model (apart from not being the best model for this data)! So, if you ever thought that generating models in the context of statistical modeling or ML is like rocket science, not really (at least, not always), it can be as easy as this example! The basic underlying concept of using **statistics** is to look at data from the past, trying to describe that data as accurately as possible (with a function). Our statistical model characterizes the **relationship** between the dates (input variable) and our sales (output variable). We call this procedure **statistical inference** (where eg. confidence intervals play a part, see chapter 2.3) instead of **prediction**. However, we can still use this model to make predictions via extrapolating this function (simply enlarging our red line furthermore) to predict future data, like tomorrow`s sales.

Summing up our last thoughts, we statistically examined our data to create a statistical sales data model to infer something about the relationships within the data. After we have found the data's pattern, we can use that relationship to predict future values. Some people think it is already ML as soon as we predict anything. However, as we have just experienced, this is not true.

In our easy example, we can also predict future values using a simple statistical model like linear regression.

Whether we will use statistical models or ML to analyze our data, one of the very first steps should always be Exploratory Data Analysis (EDA, see chapter 1.4.2), which we will use statistics for. Only if we know and understand the **shape** and **distribution** of our data will we be able to **fit** meaningful **models** to it. Knowing the data`s distribution is generally very important for statistical models, less so for ML models. The reason for this will be explained in the next chapter.

1.1.2 MACHINE LEARNING

Besides basic statistics, we will also use **machine learning** (ML) to predict our sales data. But why will we do this? Are statistical models with all their possibilities, like linear regression, exponential smoothing, etc., insufficient? What can ML put on top of basic statistics to bring any benefit to our predictions? To answer all these questions, let us first start by defining what ML is:

ML is the science of getting computers to act **without** being **explicitly programmed**.

In traditional programming, we code the rules explicitly. This means we are adding rules (like if-else statements, etc.) to receive answers from the data. In our case, we would code, e.g., the linear regression, to predict future sales. Even for this easy example, this approach already shows a big disadvantage of traditional coding: if the data changes in the future, the model will not be able to adapt to this new situation. It will just keep on sticking to its linear regression model (with its predefined parameter settings), even if the data cannot be modeled with a linear regression any longer.

ML differs from that approach: we only have to feed in the data, and the machine will figure out the rules themselves. ML is an algorithm that can learn from data without relying on rules-based programming. So even if data changes in the future, the model (the rules) will be able to adapt to this new situation and give answers to that new - but similar - data by itself. Why did we say new but similar data? Only if the new data is similar to the old data on which the model has been **trained** will the model be able to make good predictions. If the new data changed completely compared to the old data (in other words, the patterns in the data changed dramatically), then our model will likely fail to predict in a good manner. Our model`s accuracy heavily relies on the data on which the model has been trained (train data, see chapter 1.2.5).

To be more precise, the data we have to train an ML model is split into **labels** (or **targets)** and **features.** With features - often denoted using the symbol x- we mean descriptive attributes influencing the label (like sales amount). So, features are data that help us predict. Features are called independent, explanatory, or input variables in statistical modeling. In our case, date and customer are features that influence our target (label) sales amount. The label/target we are trying to predict can be labeled or unlabeled (see unsupervised ML in the next chapter) and is typically called Y (while in statistical modeling, they are called dependent, response, or output variable).

Our data set includes SalesValue (net sales) and SalesAmount (quantity sold) as targets. These targets are influenced by the features SalesDate, SalesItems, and Customer (and there could be many more, like sales discounts, sales events, etc.).

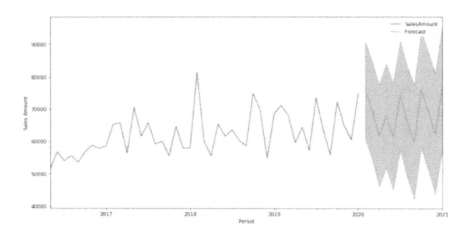

(screenshot taken from chapter 2.1)

To understand how to apply ML algorithms, it helps if we think about ML in this form:

Machine Learning = Formulation + Optimization + Evaluation

Those terms are defined as follows:

The **formulation** is about finding a clever way to describe a business problem in a way that relates to the input and output data that our ML algorithm knows how to process. This means we search for meaningful input-output data and collect and package it in the format the ML algorithm expects. Regarding our data, which we will use in chapter 2, the net sales or sales quantity is our target Y, which we want to predict using the Sales Date as a feature x. ML is furthermore separated into two major groups depending on whether we have a labeled or unlabeled dataset:

- Unsupervised machine learning
- Supervised machine learning

In **unsupervised** learning, we only have features but can't assign a target to those features. In layperson's terms, unsupervised ML mostly means clustering, while clustering is just a fancier word for grouping. "A cluster is a set of similar entities, or at a minimum, a set of entities that are more similar to each other than to members of other clusters. It's human nature to cluster things, and it's often the first step on the road to knowledge." (from The Master Algorithm: How the Quest for the Ultimate Learning Machine Will Remake Our World, by Pedro Domingos). In chapter 2, we will use an unsupervised learning algorithm to recognize groups of similar customers and assign them a label. The label itself will not give us any insights; it is up to us (humans) to understand the reason for this grouping (done by machines). In contrast, we already know what we're looking for in **supervised** learning since we have labeled our targets with features.

How can ML figure out the rules by itself?

The answer is **optimization.** In ML, we train a **model** with **data.** These features fit a function that should predict the target as accurately as possible. Put another way, the features (e.g. date) are mapped by a certain function to give us the target value y (sales value or sales amount). In ML, we use **gradient descent** for fitting a linear regression: $y = m*x + w + x2*w2 + ... + xn*wn$. The features are x, and the parameters (as we call them in ML terms, weights would be the statistic model term) are w. Until here, this is the same function as in a linear regression statistic model. However, in ML, we minimize the **cost function** (e.g., MSE, see chapter 1.2.5) by iteratively updating parameters/weights using the gradient descent technique. To understand how gradient descent works, imagine a climber on top of a mountain. For some reason, the climber now needs to go down the mountain to reach the bottom of the valley. Because of dense fog, the climber can only see the ground within a two-foot radius. To get to the valley, the climber will look at the slope of the ground around (only seeing a two-foot radius) and turn a single step in that direction, where the ground slopes most steeply downward. Afterward, the climber repeats that step again and again. Sticking to that direction of the gradient of the mountain, the climber will eventually arrive at the valley's bottom. Gradient descent starts by selecting a random point within the weight space and calculates the error measure repeatedly until the global minimum on the error surface is reached.

So optimization is the "pure" algorithm itself (what the ML algorithm does internally) to minimize the error (difference between actual and predicted values). It's the process of applying math to get an optimal solution. The optimal solution is defined according to an evaluation metric (see chapter 1.2.5). Remember that we just said that ML can figure out the rules by itself? This figuring out is nothing less than optimizing our model, and **optimizing** is what is meant by **learning** in ML.

To recap, the ML algorithm will learn the rules behind the data's patterns (if any) by itself, without any explicit coding of rules by the human. For a supervised ML algorithm to learn how to make predictions, we must show it both the inputs and the desired respective outputs. The model will then automatically extract the relationships between these inputs and outputs while trying to minimize the error (predicted value compared against actual, doing it all in one big loop until the sweet spot is found). This data set (or data points) is called **train data** and includes features **xtrain** and the target **ytrain.** By training a model on train data we are trying to predict ytrainPredicted values that nail the actual ytrain as closely as possible. This training can also be called **learning,** which is where learning in ML comes from. By comparing the predicted ytrain values against the actual ytrain values, we can calculate an **accuracy score** (or error score/ metric). But even if we set up a model that fits our train data perfectly well, does that mean we will also perfectly predict unseen data points? In other words, even if we have set up a model with an accuracy of 100% on train data, will we be able to predict, e.g., next week's targets nearly perfectly if next week's x features are very different from the x features the model has been trained on past train data? Probably not. The algorithm has a **tendency to cheat** to minimize its loss function by **overfitting** to data. Overfitting means that the model is too complex, it might have too many features with larger weights and, therefore, weak **generalization. Underfitting** is quite the opposite of overfitting: the model is too simple and has relatively fewer features with smaller weights, so we can call it a weak learning model. A "good fit" model compromises fit and complexity (drop features, reduce weights) and is achieved using **regularization.** Regularization penalizes large weights, sometimes reduced all the way to zero. This is why after learning a function based on the training set data, that is where **test data** comes into play, to strengthen the reliability of our model's forecast. Test data is data that the model has not "seen" during the training session (it is not available to the model for learning). Test Data only ensures that the model generalizes well on new "unseen" data. This "train/test" trick used in ML is not used in statistical modeling at all. Using statistical models to locate any outliers before modeling our data is vital. In ML terms this is not per se the case: usually, we want to train our model to include all the data, also with **"outliers"**. The model should learn how to deal with these data points on its own. But replacing outliers will make sense if we don't have many data points. Otherwise, we will most likely end up with a strongly overfitted model. Overfitting means our model follows the errors (or noise) too closely. It is an undesirable situation because the fit obtained will yield inaccurate estimates of the response on new observations that were not part of the original training data set.

By the way, the Machine (behind ML) does not know what a date is. It is just seeing data points in specific sequence order (indexed target). The date is simply an indexed feature x that influences our target sales amount y. Even if we extract additional outdated features (e.g., summer, winter, etc.), the Machine still does not know that summer might be sweltering (depending on where we live). But if the hot weather has some influence on our targets, our Machine should be able to find these patterns and forecast accordingly. Even if someone has lots of sophisticated ML algorithms combined and therefore is able to forecast any time series very precisely (and thus since she is very proud of her smart combination of algorithms she calls that Artificial Intelligence), the algorithms do not have an intelligence comparable to us humans. The Machine is just encoding the features, so it can understand a **correlation** between summer and sales, if there is any. Summer and sales are said to be positively correlated if high summer values go in with high sales values and low summer values go with low sales values. If high summer values come with low sales values, and vice versa, the variables are negatively correlated. ML is always just about correlation, never about **causation!** The Machine also needs to learn what sales are; it is just numbers for the Machine. Doesn`t sound too intelligent to you? I like the comparison between babies and ML very much in this case: we would teach a baby for instance what a cat is simply by showing it a cat (each pixel of the cat being a kind of feature) and calling it a cat (target). If we just repeat this often enough, the young kid one day will be very precise in categorizing a cat as a cat. That is quite similar to ML. Just feed the algorithm with enough cat pictures and label it accordingly, and the Machine will become very good at recognizing unseen cats correctly as a cat.

Sticking to our cat example, there is no "one feature cat," but hundreds of thousands of features exist. So, it is not only the distance between the eyes that identifies a cat as such, but it is the combination of many aspects (eyes, nose, mouth, ear, etc). Finally, each picture is made up of a single pixel, and how these pixels are made up defines what the picture displays. Machines are impressive in labeling multidimensional features on mass data and figuring out the patterns behind the data by themselves. That is what the term learning in ML means: the machine is very efficient in optimizing the model. So, intelligence (i.e., in artificial intelligence or learning in ML) is merely reduced to optimizing complex multidimensional models, which is very tough or even impossible for humans. For instance, if we know that seasons and discounts have an influence on sales, these two features are still quite easy for us humans to look at in an x-y diagram and spot any patterns on our own. However, as soon as we meet a three- or four-dimensional feature space, it becomes pretty challenging for our eyes to detect patterns. Now think of a 10, 20, 3000.. dimensional feature space. Humans are not able to digest this in an efficient way, but machines can!

Evaluation is the application of the evaluation metric to measure the success of the optimization. The ML aims to iteratively find the function that maps the x values to the y values with the lowest error possible (the lowest overall deviation between actual and predicted ones). We call the set of all possible functions that can describe this mapping as the hypothesis space. It's up to us as algorithm users to understand which evaluation metric is best and what the best format is for our data. Machines currently are good at the optimization point, but the other two aspects are still up to us. Only we can link the ML algorithms to our business data (and our business logic behind it), so only we can formulate and evaluate the best approach regarding parameter tuning and evaluation meaningfully.

What can ML put on top of statistic models?

ML can find patterns between input and output on its own,

and afterward, this trained model can predict future values. But where is the benefit to statistical models, where, e.g., a linear regression model is also able to predict future values? Before we answer this, let us first make sure we will not get puzzled by the different wordings for "Statistical Models" and "ML":

A statistical model can give the same result as an ML model (like we can also set up a linear regression using an ML framework). The approach is slightly different: in basic statistics, our linear regression will give us the best result in one shot because of its closed form. In ML, because of the iterative approach, the model will provide the same result when it finally hits the lowest error. The aim of ML is mostly to predict future values, that's why we use the "train-test split", which is different from any statistical model.

As a short summary, in ML the algorithm (i.e. the machine) will learn relationships from a training dataset (from the past) and then be able to apply these relationships to new data. Whereas a traditional statistical model will apply a predefined relationship (model) to forecast sales, an ML algorithm will not assume a priori a particular relationship (the parameters like a linear trend): it will learn these patterns directly from the historical data. Another important difference between using ML and, e.g., exponential smoothing models to forecast is that an ML algorithm will learn patterns from all our data. Exponential smoothing models will treat each item individually, independently of the others. An ML algorithm will learn patterns from the entire dataset and apply what works best to each sales item. One could improve the accuracy of an exponential smoothing model by increasing the length of each time series (i.e., providing more historical periods for each product). Still, with ML, we can improve our model's accuracy by providing more items. ML models are able to learn many **relationships** (e.g. derived features from our sales data like weekdays, holidays, etc) that are beyond the ability of traditional statistics. The purpose of ML is to obtain the best performance on the test set, which means it can make repeatable predictions. ML does so by trying a variety of different models and **converging** to the final hypothesis. The model must not even be **interpretable,** as long as the predictions are accurate. Some ML model is kind of black boxes (see eg. LSTM in chapter 2.3.3), while others transparently can display their inner rules (eg. decision tree, see chapter 2.3.1). Statistical modeling is more about finding relationships between variables and the significance of those relationships. In traditional statistical modeling, we select one model and can evaluate its accuracy (considering bias), but cannot automatically make it select the best model from e.g. 7 different models (see chapter 2.2). Obviously, there is always some bias in the model depending on the chosen model. A few decades ago, we did not have the large amounts of data we have today accessible. That is one reason why, in the past, we used statistical models instead of ML models. ML models often achieve better results compared to statistical models when fed with many data points. It is much easier and cheaper to produce, collect, and store data today. Secondly, we only have powerful computing resources available nowadays, which many ML models rely on. Thirdly, ML frameworks and libraries have improved and are more efficient these days (and they will continue to evolve further in the future).

Sometimes, an example app explains more than a thousand words. For a practical and easy-to-follow example, let us briefly move away from our task of analyzing sales and look at an image classification task (one of the critical areas of ML). Before further explanation, please click the link and get an unbiased first impression of this fascinating live ML model by Zaid Alyafeai:

https://www.dar-analytics.de/sketcher.html

This model has been trained with 100 sketch classes (coffee cup, smiley, snake, etc.) from the sketches repository (https://

github.com/googlecreativelab/quickdraw-dataset). When we are painting a cup, the model will label it correctly as a cup, just because it got trained with many different cup sketches before (which were labeled as cups):

Even though this app might seem a little childish, this model is a severe **Convolutional Neural Network** (CNN) which impressively can master image classification tasks (supervised). Classifying the sketches has not been explicitly hard-coded, and that's what makes ML so fascinating. Even if in the future someone paints a cup in a very different style compared to elderly-trained data cup images, the system will predict a category (and hopefully it will rank the cup as the best guess). Try to achieve that with explicit coding! Even if you try to hard code thousands of rules (explicit coding), still in the future there will be someone painting a cup in an unusual (not imagined before) way. Your hard-coded solution will likely fail, but your ML model can still correctly assume that this painting should be a cup (with the highest confidence).

I hope you`re enjoying this CNN Deep Learning App as much as my kids (and I) do. And if you also just can`t get enough of this, here is one more impressive app, this time about word vectorization (complete different task, but still an ML model) from Google:

http://projector.tensorflow.org.

And if we want to tinker more with the technical aspects of a Neural Network, this Google App is quite intuitive and helpful:

https://playground.tensorflow.org

These examples substantiate that image classification (and natural learning processing) are awe-inspiring areas of ML. In these fields, ML proves its dominance, so some people who used to have said in the past that "software is eating the world" are now saying, "ML is eating software." Even though skepticism per se is not a bad thing, I tend to say we do not need to worry about what ML might bring us in the future, rather than be "hands-on excited" and critical (see chapter 1.5). What I mean by "hands-on excited" is that I think we can only understand something – and only if we understand something can we be constructively judgeful about it- if we really get our hands on these algorithms to understand what it's all about truly. We will challenge in detail how supportive they will be for our purpose of analyzing and predicting sales, as well as recommending items to our customers. And that is exactly what we are going to do when analyzing our sales data in chapter 2.

There are so many different ML algorithms out there; sometimes it's hard to see the woods (the "random forest") for the trees (Decision Trees):

Algorithm Hub
Algorithms
ML Categories
Machine Learning (ML)

Luckily, after this chapter, we have a basic understanding of ML. We will also use a lot of algorithms in the coding of chapter 2 to clear the fog.

Let us strongly state one keynote: there would not be any ML if not for (basic) statistics. ML is built upon a statistical framework! Sometimes, we will be surprised to see that even very sophisticated ML models do not overachieve the accuracy of statistical models (e.g., exponential smoothing or linear regression). Per se, we can't tell if an ML model will result in higher accuracy against a statistical model or not. This depends on our data. In short, an ML model is the better choice if we predict a target influenced independently by **many features** (see chapter 2.2). On the other hand, if we want to describe our past data points with regards to data distribution etc. this cries out for a statistical model. No training and no test set are necessary for a statistical model (opposite to ML), but the evaluation will instead involve evaluating the significance and robustness of the model parameters, which is not mandatory for ML. We often have to try out and compare which technique gives us better results. Only afterward can we tell in which circumstances ML brings us any advantages compared to basic statistics (which some would call "old school" statistics, but that just sounds a little bit too disrespectful in my ears). In chapter 2.3, it is best practice to use basic **statistic models** as a **benchmark** against any ML models. Basic statistics also very often deals with **hypothesis** testing, something which is unusual in ML -which rather focuses on what the model predicts- but we will use it for interpreting model parameters or the meaning of fit parameters for the sake of more transparency of our ML model (see library Statsmodel in chapter 2.1).

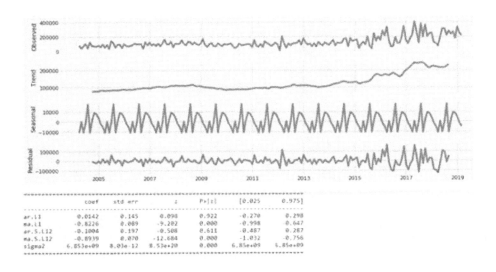

(screenshot taken from chapter 2.1)

In real-world solutions, many different models are combined to solve a task. For example, in chapter 2.3, we will first run an unsupervised model to cluster our customers. Afterward, we could run product recommendation/basket analysis on these clusters for better alignment. Now, let us go through the whole ML process in more detail.

1.2 STAIRWAY TO MACHINE LEARNING

Don`t do as I do, do as I say! (My boss used saying with a wink)

Although it is not always wise to be a slave to the process, it is sometimes helpful to stick to some best practices. Applying ML is a path from data to answering (business) questions to create value from data and usually follows these process steps:

Question (Formulation)- Data Processing- Algorithm (Evaluation)- Model and Parameter Selection (Optimization)- Result Interpretation- Deploy as an answer or data product if the result is worth it, otherwise re-train (going back to Evaluation and repeat all steps)

The toughest part of nearly all data analysis projects is receiving the right data in the right (prepared) way. This means we do not only need data, but we must ensure that we understand it. We will use Exploratory Data Analysis (EDA, see chapter 2.1) for this discovery task. On top of that, we need to link the data to our business know-how because only correct labeling ensures measurability and focus. While exploring our data during EDA, we might find missing values that we have to fill in or clean (see chapter 1.2.3.1), and we need to transform (preprocess) and data engineer our data (chapter 1.2.3.2) as the next steps. Even though there are already libraries (like auto-sklearn or Dabl) that try to automate these steps, it's still the human who teaches the machine. There will be no free lunch! No single method by default dominates all others, but executing the best solution is always strongly data-dependent. Data quality is critical and usually always improves during an ML journey. Data cleansing and evaluating results may not sound too sexy - even though Harvard Business Review says Data Science is the sexiest job of the 21st century - but will probably take a significant part of our capacity during our whole analysis project. But, preparing data is worth the effort because quality data is more important than using complicated algorithms and will surely turn to account in the long run.

The question of what **algorithm** to select mostly depends on our data and the question we are trying to answer with it. Even slight changes in our data set might lead to other methods working better afterward than the previous solution on a similar data set. Hence, deciding which model for a defined task produces the best results for any given set of data is essential. Selecting the best approach can be a challenging part of performing ML in practice, but will come in with improved maintainability compared to heuristics and rules over rules. After choosing the suitable model, we have to decide about the model parameters for our project (see chapters 1.2.4 and 2.2). Finally, after fitting our model with our data, we need to benchmark the results and choose the model (including model parameters) that achieved the best results (1.2.5). There is no artificial intelligence (AI) yet, which we can simply throw in any data and automatically compute meaningful results out of it in a self-learning way! However, we do have to evaluate our results (translate the results into our business reality) and integrate the best settings into our processes and systems. This will come in with higher value by automation and increased usability.

After all this hard work, we are proud as heck and want to share our results with the world (okay, at least with our colleagues). Therefore, we should consider what tool to use to

broadcast our ML model results. This book's coding chapter will stick to Jupyter Notebook and Excel exports. But in your company, you might decide to use business intelligence tools for better usability. If our recipients accept our results, we will move our ML model into a productive environment where we must constantly challenge our results. If data trends change over time, we must adapt our model with the current data, re-training and re-deploying our model. Let us now have a closer look at the steps nearly all ML projects go through. I understand if some of the topics are not natural right away if you have never heard of them before. But we will catch the intuition behind these latest during our coding exercise in chapter 2.

1.2.1 DATA FORMULATION

It`s the data, stupid! (originally coined "It`s the economy, stupid!" by James Carville for Bill Clinton`s presidential campaign in 1992)

Since Data is the most fundamental aspect of any analysis, let us take the time to understand the many different data formats. We will later see that this is time well spent since understanding metadata is often crucial for many of the algorithms we will use.

Where is data housed (data storage)?

Often, data is stored in a database, where you can access nicely formatted and prepared **fact** and **dimension** tables. Since this book does not discuss **data warehouses** (DWH) in detail, we will not go any deeper here. But if you are interested in data warehousing, I recommend reading Ralph Kimball's books about that topic.

Besides comfortably prepared fact and dimension tables stored in a BI layer in a data warehouse, the concept of a **data lake** also exists. AWS (Amazon Web Services) states a data lake is "a centralized repository that allows you to store all your **structured** and **unstructured** data at any scale. You can store your data as-is without having to structure it first." So, a data lake is a very compelling addition to data warehouses. As a system or repository of data stored in its natural/raw format, usually object blobs or files, a data lake can include structured not only data from relational databases (rows and columns) but also semi-structured data (CSV, logs, JSON, XML) unstructured data (emails, documents, pdf) and binary data (images, audio, video).

What does data look like?

Data can come in handy as a data warehouse table (loaded with data, e.g., out of a transactional db, like an ERP system), an Excel, CSV, text, etc. All of them have one thing in common: they are all **tabular** data. That is data that is nicely **structured** in tables with rows and columns. Just think of the lists and tables we use, e.g., an Excel spreadsheet. Structured data depends on a data model and resides in a fixed field within a record. Storing structured data in tables within databases or Excel/Access files is often straightforward. SQL (Structured Query Language) is the preferred way to manage and query structured data in databases. We will only give a short introduction on how to pull data out of a database using SQL, but if you need more details about **SQL,** please check for other sources since that is out of this book's scope: SQL is a crucial skill every analyst must have at one's disposal.

Even though structured data is always about rows and columns, there might still be tweaks to it. This tabular data can be a lovely flat table, or your measure is split into many columns. Depending on the algorithm you will use, you need to melt/ unstack your data first (more details in chapter 2.1). The data we will use in Chapter 2 is structured data, which comes in handy in a clean **flat table**, but we will demonstrate some data massaging examples anyway.

In real life, more often, data comes in **unstructured.** Unstructured data is complex to fit into a data model because the content varies. One example of unstructured data is regular email. An email does contain structured elements such as the sender and title. However, each human will write a specific body text, even if the content of the email is about the same topic. Everyone writes differently, and there are many different languages out there. Hence, an email is one example of unstructured data used for natural language processing (NLP).

Everything in between these two structures is called **semistructured** data. According to Wikipedia, semistructured data is "a form of structured data that does not obey the tabular structure of data models associated with relational databases or other forms of data tables, but nonetheless contains tags or other markers to separate semantic elements and enforce hierarchies of records and fields within the data. Therefore, it is also known as a self-describing structure." In semistructured data, the entities belonging to the same class may have different attributes even though they are grouped, and the attributes' order is not essential. Semistructured data is increasingly occurring because the Internet's rich documents and databases are no longer the only forms of data. But we will see a lot of JSON and XML files for exchange. Sometimes, structured data is also complex to store in relational databases, such as hierarchical data (e.g., a company's organizational chart).

The **data** itself, which we are going to use to run our sales analysis, can furthermore be **classified** into two groups:

Endogenous is input data (e.g., our sales data from the past), and **exogenous** is further divided into **internal** (sales events, price discounts, promotions, etc.) and **external** (weather, GDP, Covid-19..) exogenous data. On the last level, our data can be classified by the **data types**, which are basically (regarding structured data) numeric, categorical, or interval. **Numeric** (numeric values allow arithmetic operations) data comes either as **continuous** (such as sales value) or **discrete** (e.g., the count of the occurrence of sales events). **Categorical** (a finite set of values that cannot be ordered and do not allow arithmetic operations) data takes only a fixed set of values, such as, e.g., **textual** (free form text) sales region (north, east, west, south). **Binary** data (a set of just two values) is a critical particular case of categorical data. One such example is the occurrence of a sales transaction, which we will use for our market basket analysis (see Chapter 2.4). We only count if a customer has bought a specific item yet, so it can only take one of two values (has bought yes or has not bought. So whenever you see a yes/no, 0/1, or true/false column, that is binary. Another type of categorical data is **ordinal** data (which, in contrast to numeric, allows ordering but does not permit arithmetic operations) in which the categories are ordered. One example is our numerical rating for top recommended items per customer (Top1, Top2, Top3, etc., see Chapter 2.5). Sales Date is one example of **interval** data, which does allow ordering and subtraction but no other arithmetic calculations.

Since these data types play an essential role for both statistical and machine learning models, let us now have a look at which data types Python has built-in by default:

Text Type: Str (like Customer Name)

Numeric Types: int, float (like Sales Amount), complex

Sequence Types: list, tuple, range

Mapping Type: Dict (data storage structure, which contains a list of key-value paired elements)

Set Types: set, frozenset (immutable version of a set)

Boolean Type: Bool (like "purchased yes" vs "purchased no")

Binary Types: bytes, bytearray, memoryview

Why are data types so vital that we look at them in such detail?

One apparent reason is that you cannot calculate with strings but only on numerical values (like integers). But there are more reasons – maybe not as evident at first glance- regarding data types, which can lead to errors when used with algorithms. Let us think of marks we received back in school. Mark 1 was the best result, while Mark 6 was the worst. So, mark 2 is not as perfect as mark 1. But mark 2 is still a good mark and better than mark 3 (and therefore also better than marks 4,5 and 6). We see that these marks follow a logic scale. In contrast, let us think of specific clusters 1,2, 3, and 4 that do not obey any logical sorting order. One example would be if your data is separated into North, West, South, and East. First, we cannot always feed these strings directly to a model. Instead, we must map them to numeric values representing strings as a one-hot vector (see chapter 2.2). Second, after we have mapped North to 1, South to 2, West to 3, and East to 4, these numbers do not have a more profound logic behind them. We cannot say that 2 (South) > 1 (North). We must consider this before feeding any models. Otherwise, our results might be misleading or may run into errors.

In ML, **balanced** and **imbalanced** data can play an important role. For instance, if you want to train a classifier to separate between "will buy next week" and "will not buy next week," a fair approach would be using 50% of the data for "yes" and the other 50% data should be "no" datasets. That dataset would be called a balanced data set. But if you -for whatever reasons- should have 80% yes and only 20% no datasets available, that data set would be imbalanced. That will significantly influence your ML model simply because the "no" class is poorly underrepresented, which can lead to bias in your model. A simple solution to this problem would be to select more "no" data sets to fit the model with a balanced 50% / 50% ratio. Or decrease the number of the "yes" classes if you still have enough data sets afterward. That is quite simple, but if we think of a more critical task -fraud detection- most of our datasets will usually be labeled as nonfraud (say 98% of all our datasets). Only a minimal amount of datasets are labeled as fraud, hopefully (2%). So, when you train your model without further cross-checking, you might quickly end up with a 98% accuracy. At first glance, we might be happy about this "naïve" result, but after having a deeper look, we understood that our model always predicts any dataset as fraud.

Does size matter?

What about the **size of data** sets (the number of data points/ rows)? The more data we have, the better? Well, it depends: more features does not necessarily mean it'll help us improve our model **(curse of dimensionality**, leading to overfitting, see chapter 1.2.1). The curse of dimensionality means that the volume of the **feature space** increases so fast that the available data becomes **sparse.** This sparsity is problematic with regard to statistical significance because the amount of data needed to support the result must grow exponentially with the dimensionality. This sparsity will also make clustering very inefficient (or even impossible). But usually, we can say, "The more data points, the better." Nowadays, you can read a lot about big data in the media. But the term big here is relative and should be understood as being difficult data. Difficult because it is hard to extract value from and costly to manage. Difficult also because of the sheer size of the data volume. We will not touch big data in our coding part (our dataset fits into a simple Excel file), but if you should ever encounter that your data does not fit into memory any longer using a Pandas data frame (df), it will be your starting point to turn to PySpark. A df is just indexed rectangular (a two-dimensional matrix with rows and columns) data similar to an Excel spreadsheet and is the basic data structure for statistical and ML models (we will deal with df a lot; see all coding chapters). When coding, we will see that with smaller datasets, an easier approach (like, for instance, a decision tree) can overachieve a complex neural network (see chapter 2.3.3).

What if there is not enough data around?

Depending on our project, we can use data **augmentation** or **feature engineering** (see chapter 1.2.3.2). Sticking to already **pre-trained** models is not a solution for us since our sales time series data is so company-unique (in all likelihood) that we will not find models that have already been trained on our individual sales data.

Now that we understand the metadata of our data let us explore it further.

1.2.2 EXPLORATORY DATA ANALYSIS

We need to ensure that our data is suitable for answering our business question before we try to build and train any model. Thus, we have to dive deeper into understanding the project`s aim, and we also have to try to think outside the box from the start. Does diving deeper and thinking outside the box sound like the opposite to you? What I mean by that is pondering the algorithm details comes later. At the beginning of our project, we had to concentrate first on our main aim, not the granular coding aspects. Algorithm and model details are coming later, not the other way around, since otherwise, that will most likely only cost us additional recurrent work. I think, and that is not only due to my personal experiences, that we will likely get lost in ML details (like model parameter selection and tuning) way too early. This is very understandable since we want to push things forward. We are too keen on getting ML models under our fingertips since we want to come to the thrilling lion`s dent as soon as possible. But please let me give you this advice- which I had to learn the hard way more than once- to take more time on your business question and the data that comes with it before training any models. For instance, does our sales data have what it takes to run product recommendations? Exploratory Data Analysis (EDA) will help us understand our data to see if it is fruitful data for answering our (business) question. EDA is one approach to analyzing a dataset and capturing its main characteristics, using univariate statistics like histograms, (Box)

Plots, etc.. Using EDA, we can discover our data visually for any apparent patterns or anomalies, check assumptions, and test hypotheses.

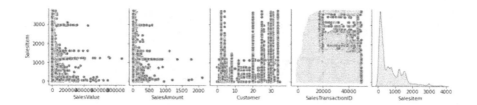

(screenshot taken from chapter 2.1)

Only after we have seriously examined our data are we able to decide which algorithm to try out. Data will dominate the model we choose, not the other way around!

1.2.3 DATA WRANGLING

Now that we understand the shape and distribution of our data, thanks to EDA in the previous step, we can use the knowledge we gathered to prepare the data for ML algorithms. That means we can start preparing our data to set up an ML model. For instance, during EDA, we spotted that NaN (NaN, not a number, Python`s equivalent to null) values exist in our dataset. Since not all ML models can deal with NaN values, we must do something about it (saying we must prepare it). But organizing and cleaning in the sense of deleting missing datasets also meant gathering, integrating, restructuring, transforming, loading, filtering, deleting, combining, merging, verifying, extracting, shaping, and massaging it. All these are necessary because, in the real world, data rarely comes in as numerical data in a tidy labeled features format, which ML models need it to be. As we will see in chapter 2.5.3, sometimes we need our data to be in a tabular format for a specific algorithm (e.g., decision tree), while for Apriori Market Basket analysis in chapter 2.4.1, we will use a sales transaction id/item matrix to run our algorithm on.

As soon as we have the required data at our fingertips, let's examine the most common data quality issues before we can train an ML model.

1.2.3.1 DATA CLEANING

There are two types of people in this world: those who can extrapolate from incomplete data! (author unknown)

If we have **erroneous** or **missing** values in our data, we must either delete that data point (or, in some cases, drop the whole feature) or replace it (e.g., with a mean value of other data points). Please note that you cannot per se tell what approach makes the most sense, but that strongly depends on your dataset and goal. In some cases, it will make sense to replace a missing value just with the median or (moving) average value (maybe think of stock prices). Still, in other cases, chances are too high that a mean cannot replace the missing value because the **volatility** in the dataset is just too high for that approach. Before leading to **bias** in your model, you should delete this missing data point to prevent your model from sitting on the wrong track.

1.2.3.2 DATA PREPARATION

Besides NaN (not a number), many models also do not work well with **non-numerical** data like **categorical** data, so we must first **transform** categorical values into numerical values. Instead of a customer name like "customer Harry," we have to map this customer to a customer Code "1". There are several strategies to handle categorical features, like creating a dictionary to map categorical values to numerical ones. After our algorithm finishes the calculation on this customer code, we can eventually map the customer code number 1 back to its original customer name, so we can see that customer1 stands for customer Harry (instead of using the vacuous code 1).

This numerical mapping is not always a good approach (at least not for all algorithms). In Scikit-Learn, the model assumes that numerical features reflect algebraic quantities. That implies that 1<2<3.. etc, or even worse: 3-2 equals 1, which, of course, is complete nonsense regarding our customers (the ordering and size of the integers are, in fact, meaningless).

Luckily, we can use a technique called **One-Hot-Encoding** to solve this problem, which explodes the categorical features into many binary features (as many categories as each feature has). In other words, it creates extra columns for each category, including binary data (0 if the category is not matching, 1 if matching, that's why "one-hot"). Get_Dummies is the pandas One-Hot-Encoder, which converts categorical features into new "dummy"/ indicator features. For One-Hot Encoding of only one feature alone, we shall use LabelBinarizer instead. If you want to use them, remember to map them to your df (data frame).

To convert a category into a numeric, use the "Categorical-cat. codes" function (see chapter 2.1).

We have just translated strings into numbers for computational reasons so the algorithm can work with these. If we have dozens of categories, training a model on one-hot encodings becomes computationally too heavy. Embedded columns are a solution to overcome this. Instead of representing the data as a one-hot vector of many dimensions, an embedding column means that the data is a **lower-dimensional**, **dense vector** in which each cell can contain any number, not just 0 or 1. The size of the embedding is a parameter that must be tuned. If the encoded data contains mostly zeros, **sparse matrices** can also be an efficient solution (see chapter 2.5.3).

By changing the values to fall within a specified range while maintaining the relative differences between the values, we ensure equal importance before training any model with it. This technique is called **normalization** (see chapter 2.5.3). Using Matrix Factorization during chapter 2.5.6 **(vectorization)**, we will convert data into well-behaved vectors.

What we have done (while mapping a number to a non-number category like customers, but this technique is also used for representing images or texts in ML) is called **feature extraction** (like encoding vectorization..). That is close to **feature engineering** (multiplication, squaring, polynomial features, loss, etc.). Feature engineering is about reshaping our data into features that better represent the underlying structure of our data (called transformation in statistical modeling). Feature engineering is sometimes called feature deriving (mathematically deriving a new feature from an existing one), which is used to extract more features from the original dataset to increase our model's accuracy (increasing the model's complexity) and imputation of missing data. Even with our minimal dataset (limited to the number of targets and features, which are only five columns overall), we can already calculate **Key Performance Indicators** (KPI). KPI are calculated/ aggregated/ derived measures. By transforming the raw data into numbers, we can use these numbers to build our feature matrix suitable for our ML model (in other words, for preparing our data for the model).

On the other hand, feature engineering is also used to create novel features. The intuition behind it is to think about what information a human would use to predict, using domain knowledge and sometimes good old **try and error**. Or do you prefer to call it brute-forcing?

Let's assume there was a clear seasonal pattern in our sales data regarding summer and winter. Since we only have SalesDate as a field, we will extract a new feature out of SalesDate, calling that feature "season" (winter or summer). In the end, we always have to check if our extracted or engineered features optimizes our model via **feature selection (dimensionality reduction)**:

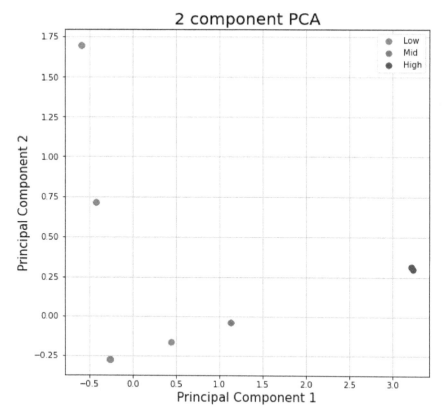

(screenshot taken from chapter 2.2)

This has three reasons:

- Dimensionality reduction due to **curse of dimensionality**
- Improved visualization
- Performance improvement for the ML computation

To get rid of these pitfalls, one very well-known technique is called **principal component analysis** (PCA). PCA uses the data`s variance as a criterion to sort the features. The idea is to find the coordinate axis in the feature space with the highest variance. The other axes are sorted by decreasing variance, except that all axes have to be orthogonal to each other. In doing so, we get a completely new coordinate system with a whole new **feature space**. PCA is often used for feature exploration and data visualization since we can use this technique to transform our data from high dimensional to low dimensional (only 2 or 3 dimensions) without a significant loss of information. This is because a 2- or 3-dimensional chart is way easier to digest for humans than a 10-dimensional feature space. However, PCA is also used for feature engineering, trying to result in better forecasts on test data overall. We will use these techniques in chapter 2.2 to see if our data is clustered in specific areas.

Why are we deriving new features at all?

On one hand, a pure measure usually gives us the most detail. But often, many different features influence our target, which we want to predict as accurately as possible. Suppose we use very detailed measures to predict future sales. In that case, the result will often be far from achieved values (observed) simply due to noise and error in our data (and, therefore, in our model).

On the contrary, we will highly overfit our model on our train data but fail to predict well in the future (test data). So predicting targets using more aggregated KPI figures – even though generating more "averaged" values results in higher loss than the pure measures themselves- could result in better predictions. In other words, aggregated values and "averaged clusters" often hits the target closer than pseudo-precise measures. This quickly leads to a highly **overfitted** (high variance in our model) model, which cannot generalize from past data appropriately. This might sound counterintuitive at first, but it is a fact how ML often behaves. However, we also need to ensure we do not **underfit** the model (there is a **high bias** in our model), which would mean missing the data's real fit. It is the proverbial fine line.

Data munging is often an iterative process since the data processing requirements are dependent on the algorithm (alias, the ML model). The deeper we mine our data, the more knowledge we gain, which sometimes leads us to re-run already conducted steps with revised parameters or tweaks. That is why it is good practice to always store our original dataset (data frame in pandas) untouched, so we can easily re-run steps without reimporting our data all the time.

1.2.4 MODEL OPTIMIZATION

Even for experts, it takes work to answer which **model** will give us the best guess, e.g., predicting sales as precisely as possible (see chapter 2.3). The hands-on approach to this question is often to try many promising ML models and find the one with the highest accuracy/precision. Thanks to Python, we can run this in a scalable and repetitive way (see chapter 2.2):

```
from sklearn.linear_model import LogisticRegression
from sklearn.naive_bayes import GaussianNB
from sklearn.ensemble import RandomForestClassifier
from sklearn.tree import DecisionTreeClassifier
from sklearn.svm import SVC
#create an array of models
models = []
models.append(("LR",LogisticRegression()))
models.append(("NB",GaussianNB()))
models.append(("RF",RandomForestClassifier()))
models.append(("SVC",SVC()))
models.append(("Dtree",DecisionTreeClassifier()))
models.append(("XGB",xgb.XGBClassifier()))


#measure the accuracy
for name,model in models:
    kfold = KFold(n_splits=2, random_state=22)
    cv_result = cross_val_score(model,X_train,y_train, cv = kfold,scoring = "accuracy")
    print(name, cv_result)

LR [0.14285714 0.          ]
NB [0.42857143 0.66666667]
RF [0.42857143 0.66666667]
SVC [0.28571429 0.33333333]
Dtree [0.42857143 0.5        ]
XGB [0.14285714 0.5        ]
```

(screenshot taken from chapter 2.2)

When setting up a model, the first thing is to choose a **class of model**, e.g., XGBClassifier (more about classes, modules, and packages in chapter 1.6.2):

import **xgboost** as **xgb**
models.append(("XGB",xgb.XGBClassifier()))

A class of a model is not the same as an instance of a model. These are **hyperparameters** (sometimes just called **parameters** or **instances**) we have to choose for our model, e.g., max_depth and min_child:

xgb_model   =   xgb.XGBClassifier(max_depth=3, min_child_weihgt=1)

Parameters that are important for optimizing the algorithm's performance are called hyperparameters. These are the parameters of ML algorithms that affect the algorithms' structure and the models' performance. Of course, we always seek to find the "best" set of model parameters, called model training or **optimization.** The model parameters are just numbers embedded in a model that can predict the labels (called weights in statistical modeling). **Hyperparameter tuning** looks for the best combination of hyperparameters combinations that maximizes model performance:

```
from sklearn.model_selection import GridSearchCV
param_test1 = {
 'max_depth':range(3,10,2),
 'min_child_weight':range(1,6,2)
}
gsearch1 = GridSearchCV(estimator = xgb.XGBClassifier(),
param_grid = param_test1, scoring='accuracy',n_jobs=-1,iid=False, cv=2)
gsearch1.fit(X_train,y_train)
gsearch1.best_params_, gsearch1.best_score_

({'max_depth': 3, 'min_child_weight': 1}, 0.39285714285714285)
```

(screenshot taken from chapter 2.2)

These are examples of the critical choices to make once the model class is chosen. We always fit the model to the data, not the data to the model. If our data is garbage, our model will likely also be garbage. Hyperparameters are often selected by passing values at model instantiation to search for the combination of best-fitting parameters. Usually, we have to optimize more than one hyperparameter, and hyperparameters do not tend to be independent of each other, which makes this task even trickier. Even though sometimes intuition and experience will help us a little, we often have to try out which combinations result best. Therefore, we can use the **grid search** (the CV stands for cross-validation). Sklearn's basic hyperparameter tuning method finds the optimum combination of hyperparameters by an exhaustive search over specific parameter values (using fit.predict()). We will list a few different parameter values and iterate through all the possible combinations in chapter 2.3. Sometimes, we will only realize details in our dataset later, forcing us to amend our instances (parameters) afterward. In this case, we have to go back to the appropriate step of data wrangling and repeat this step with revised settings this time.

In comparison, **training** the model after all that pre-work is done is relatively easy and straightforward. It is just a tiny fit(X_train, y_train) function, and could look like this:

xgb_model   =   xgb.XGBClassifier(max_depth=3, min_child_weihgt=1).fit(X_train, y_train)

Are you also astonished that the most thrilling part of ML seems to be the most unspectacular? So unspectacular, I have not even granted the learning a chapter for itself? That is indeed the case! You've come a long way collecting and wrangling your data, so now lean back and let the machine do the job of learning from your prepared data!

After **fitting** the model to the training data, we can predict values. In other words, we can use the model to predict labels for new data:

```
y_Pred_Train=xgb_model.predict(X_train)
y_Pred_Test=xgb_model.predict(X_test)
```

Concluding the uncertainty in such internal model parameters is not what ML algorithms are about too much. Interpreting model parameters via, e.g., statsmodels is much more a statistical modeling question mentioned in chapter 1.1.1. In ML, the proof is in optimizing the error. If our ML model is any good (also proven against test data), the ML model has accomplished its main mission with distinction, albeit we do not always understand its inner model details. In the next chapter, we will determine how to evaluate the model's performance.

1.2.5 MODEL EVALUATION

Essentially, all models are wrong, but some are useful (George Box)

Our data are sales from the past. We aim to forecast sales in the next month (future demand). We chose a model and its hyperparameters and trained it to fit the data. To determine if our trained model is useful, we need to validate that our model and hyperparameters fit the data well.

As a basic **validation,** it is good practice to benchmark our ML model against a **simple heuristic**. Only if our ML model is better than our "best simple guess" (e.g., moving average for forecasting of time series) is our ML model beneficial. Sometimes, we will be surprised (or even frustrated) to see that after working hard on improving a sophisticated CNN, the results are not significantly better than those of an exponential smoothing statistical model.

If our ML overachieves our simple heuristic, we'll benchmark our ML results in more depth. Therefore, we are separating our data into **train** and **test** data to evaluate our model's predictive power. Splitting our data into train (e.g., 80% of the data) and test (e.g., 20% of the data, which the model will not see during training) is one of the most commonly used validation strategies. The trick here is that by validating this model, we do not want to use data that the model has already been "seen" (trained on using train data). Because many ML models are good at learning our train data by heart, it's often not that difficult to achieve a match (predicted values vs actual values) of nearly 100%. Instead, we feed new data to the model (so-called test data or **hold-out test** set) and let the model label it (e.g., predict the sales). Then, we take the achieved actual train y (which the model has not been fed with before) and compare that against our prediction on test data targets. This is the same as we did with train data, but only on unseen test data this time. Hopefully, our estimations of the test data are very close to the actual target value overall. If the test data accurately represents what will come in as future data, our model can predict the future well. A good model has two properties: it has good **predictive power** (regarding train data) and **generalizes** well to data it hasn't seen (related to test data).

If we achieve good performance on the training databpoor generalization of test data, we call that **overfitting**. **Underfitting,** on the other hand, means poor performance on the training data and poor generalization on test data. Of course, there are error metrics that tell us how well our estimation matched the actual target value.

We will let our model predict on our training data and compare the predictions to the known actual values. We are measuring how well our predictions matched the indeed observed data. The **"distance"** between the **actual** and the **predicted** value is our evaluation metric on **train** data (and also on test data, in a later step). Depending on what we are trying to predict, there are two different approaches: classification and regression predictions. An algorithm that is capable of learning a classification (binary, like "purchases yes" or "purchases no," etc.) predictive model is called a classification algorithm, while trying to predict, e.g., floats like net sales next month, we have to use regression models.

For **classification** models, instruments like the **confusion** matrix are helpful and reliable analysis tools for capturing what happens in an evaluation test. It is a table showing the relation between correct predictions and types of incorrect predictions.

When we are trying to predict if a customer will buy next week or not (binary target), there are just four outcomes when the model makes a prediction: we speak of **true positive** if an instance in the test set had a positive target and was also predicted as having a positive target feature. If an instance in the test set had a negative target and was predicted to have a negative target value, that prediction is also correct and called a **true negative**. A **false positive**, on the other hand, is predicted as a positive, while actually, the target is negative. Lastly, a **false negative** predicts a negative while it is a positive value.

```
from sklearn.metrics import classification_report
print (classification_report(y_test, y_pred))

              precision    recall  f1-score   support

           0       1.00      0.50      0.67         2
           6       0.50      1.00      0.67         1
           7       1.00      1.00      1.00         1

    accuracy                           0.75         4
   macro avg       0.83      0.83      0.78         4
weighted avg       0.88      0.75      0.75         4
```

(screenshot taken from chapter 2.2)

Precision: the number of true positives is divided by all positive predictions. What percent of our predictions were correct, in layman's words? Precision is also called positive predictive value. It is a measure of a classifier's exactness. Low precision indicates a high number of false positives. The precision of a class defines how trustable the result is when the model answers that a point belongs to that class. Precision is the ratio of correctly predicted positive observations to the total predicted positive observations. Consider a dataset where a model predicts 50 examples, 45 of which are true and five false positives. We can calculate the precision for this model as follows:

Precision = TruePositives / (TruePositives + FalsePositives)

Precision = 45 / (45 + 5) = 90%

Recall: the number of true positives is divided by the number of positive values in the test data. In other words, it is about sensitivity, while it shows how well the model is able to detect a class. Recall is equivalent to a true positive rate. It is a measure of a classifier's completeness. Low recall indicates a high number of false negatives. Both precision and recall can assume values between 0 and 1. Higher values indicate better model performance.

The **F1** score is a weighted harmonic mean of precision and recall. The F1 score of a class is given by the harmonic mean of precision and recall (2x (precision * recall)/(precision+recall)). It is called harmonic because it tends toward smaller values and is less sensitive to significant outliers. F1 scores are lower than accuracy measures as they embed precision and recall into their computation. As a rule of thumb, the weighted average of F1 should be used to compare classifier models, not global accuracy.

Precision, recall, and F1 work best when dealing with binary prediction targets.

Support is the number of actual occurrences of the class in the specified dataset (see chapter 2.4.1). Imbalanced support in the training data may indicate structural weaknesses in the reported scores of the classifier and could indicate the need for stratified sampling or rebalancing. Support doesn't change between models but instead diagnoses the evaluation process.

Accuracy can only be used on classification tasks, not on regressions. Accuracy is a good measure, but only when you have symmetric datasets where values of false positives and false negatives are almost identical. Accuracy Example: if a classification predictive model made five predictions and three of them were correct, and two of them were incorrect, then the classification accuracy of the model based on just these predictions would be:

accuracy = correct predictions / total predictions

accuracy = 3 / 5 = 60%.

For a given class, the different combinations of recall and precision have the following meanings:

- High recall + high precision: the class is perfectly handled by the model

- Low recall + high precision: the model cannot detect the class well but is highly trustable when it does

- High recall + low precision: the class is well detected but the model also include points of other classes in it

- Low recall + low precision: the class is poorly handled by the model

The **classification error rate** is the percentage of observations in the test data set that our model mislabeled. The lower, the better.

One of the most common known error measures for **regression** (continuous) problems is the mean absolute error (**MAE**). MAE measures the average magnitude of the errors in a set of predictions without considering their direction. It's the average of absolute differences between prediction and actual observation over the test sample, where all individual differences have equal weight.

In contrast to MAE, the mean squared error (**MSE**) measures the average of the squares of the errors: the average squared difference between the actual values and what has been predicted.

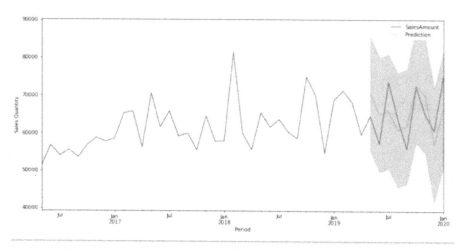

```
y_forecasted = pred.predicted_mean
y_truth = daily_df['2019-05-01':]
mse = ((y_forecasted - y_truth) ** 2).mean()
print('The Mean Squared Error of our forecasts is {}'.format(round(mse, 2)))
```

(screenshot taken from chapter 2.3)

The MSE measures the quality of an estimator. It is always non-negative due to squaring, and the smaller the MSE, the closer we are to finding the line of best fit (predicted responses are close to the actuals). The MSE will be large if, for some of the observations, the predicted and true responses differ substantially. This means that the MSE gives more weight to larger differences.

Root mean square error (**RMSE**) is the standard deviation of the residuals (prediction errors). Residuals are a measure of how far from the regression line data points are, so RMSE is a measure of how spread out these residuals are. It tells us how concentrated the data is around the line of best fit.

```
import numpy as np
print('The Root Mean Squared Error of our forecasts is {}'.format(round(np.sqrt(mse), 2)))
```

Splitting data into train and test data is probably the simplest form of sampling we can use and usually performs well on large datasets. But when we use, e.g., decision trees, we are prone to overfitting because we are iteratively building complex models and, therefore, become more and more fitted to the nuances of the train data. To avoid this, we add a third layer to our **validation** strategy called validation (train-validate-test). The validation data is used as a kind of extra train data, to tune particular aspects. Train data is used to set up the model.

In contrast, validation data helps to finetune parameters, and test data still exists to evaluate the expected performance of the model on future unseen data after deployment. There are two downsides arising from using hold-out sampling. First, our dataset must be large enough; otherwise, the evaluation results can become meaningless. Second, splitting our datasets into train-(validation)-test only once can be misleading if - by chance- the "easy" datasets will fall into the test and the "difficult" datasets are used for train. To avoid this, we can use **k-fold** cross-validation as a sampling method. The available data is divided into k equal-sized folds, and k separate evaluations are run on these partitions.

In the first run, the data in the first fold is used as test data, and the remaining folds are used as the train data. After that, in a second cycle, we take the data from the second fold as test data, and the remaining folds are then used as train data. This process continues until k is reached. For each cycle, evaluation measures are recorded, and finally, the k sets of evaluation measures (performance) are aggregated to give one overall performance measure.

We will always deal with bias when dealing with a classification or regression task. Bias is the simplifying assumptions made by the model to make the target function easier to approximate. Variance is the amount that the estimate of the target function will change given different training data. Since the training data are used to fit the model, different training data sets will result in various errors. But ideally, the estimate should not vary too much between training sets. However, if a method has high variance, small changes in the training data can result in significant changes in the error function. To minimize the expected test error, we must select a method that simultaneously achieves low variance and bias. Note that variance is inherently a nonnegative quantity, and squared bias is also nonnegative. Hence, the expected test MSE can never lie below variance, an irreducible error.

Which error metrics to choose?

Generally, **MAE** aims at the median while RMSE aims at the average. That is why EDA is so important: we have to know the distribution of our data (the median is less influenced by outliers than the mean). MAE is a bad KPI to use for **intermittent** sales (e.g., if more than half of the sales or purchases are without any sales or purchases, then the optimal forecast would be 0, which is obviously not ideal).

In general, more flexible statistical methods have higher variance. On the other hand, bias refers to the error introduced by approximating a real-life problem, which may be highly complicated by a much simpler model. If the true function f is substantially non-linear, so no matter how many training observations we are given, it will not be possible to produce an accurate estimate using linear regression. In other words, linear regression results in high bias. As a general rule, as we use more flexible methods, the variance will increase, and the bias will decrease. The relative rate of change of these two quantities determines whether the test MSE increases or decreases. As we increase the flexibility of a class of methods, the bias tends to decrease faster than the variance increases initially.

Consequently, the expected test MSE declines. However,

increasing flexibility has little impact on the bias at some point but starts to increase the variance significantly. When this happens, the test MSE increases. Good test set performance of a statistical learning method requires low variance and low squared bias. This is referred to as a **tradeoff** because it is easy to obtain a method with shallow bias but high variance (for instance, by drawing a curve that passes through every single training observation) or a technique with very low variance but high bias (by fitting a horizontal line to the data). Finding the "best model" is finding a sweet spot in the tradeoff between bias and variance. The challenge lies in finding a method for which both the variance and the squared bias are low. The mean squared error measures how big the average error of our prediction is. Squaring the average error has two consequences: you can't cancel out a wrong prediction in one direction with a faulty prediction in the other direction. For example, overestimating future sales for the next month by 5,000 doesn't cancel out underestimating it by 5,000 for the following month. As a second consequence of squaring, more considerable errors get even more weight than they otherwise would. Minor errors remain small or can even shrink, whereas significant errors are enlarged and will draw our attention. ML has many modeling techniques, and the question is which one is the right one to use.

Depending on our results, we might need to return to model selection and model parameter tuning. We can repeat this circle until we have found the perfect model for our data. If our model should underperform, there are several ways to proceed:

Model and parameter tuning:

we need to return to our model and use a more/less sophisticated or more/less flexible model and/or model parameter setting. This step is often puzzling since sometimes, even adding data points to our test data will decrease our model`s accuracy. Sometimes, minor changes to the model`s parameters significantly influence the error. The only advice I can give here is to try it out and compare the results to the most meaningful error metrics for your data analysis goal.

Data related issues:

Maybe we haven't received enough data points to make accurate predictions. We might need to add more data points or features to our target. We can achieve this by adding extra datasets or feature engineering (see chapter 2.2).

Long story short:

If we want to do ML, we will need data, formulate that data, optimize a model, and evaluate the results as long as we have found the best-fitting model's parameters.

1.3 AI, ML, DL, DS

It is what it is (Michelle Obama during the DNC´s opening night, August 2020)

Artificial Intelligence (AI) is probably the biggest buzzword we face during our sales analysis journey (maybe besides Big Data, see chapter 1.2.1). AI and ML are closely related, but behind all the excitement (sometimes even hype), AI is just a discipline of which ML is a subset. Ultimately, AI always uses algorithms that are part of ML, a toolset for realizing AI. As we just discovered in the previous chapter, ML is a method of training algorithms so that they can learn how to make decisions. ML allows computers to learn an underlying pattern in data independently, without being explicitly programmed with prior knowledge of those data patterns beforehand. We have also already made clear that ML is not a magical box that you feed data and somehow produces impressive results. Instead, ML uses various algorithms—a sequence of predefined steps—that make an answer while trying to minimize the error. In plain English, we could also say that our model tries to predict the values as closely as possible, looping through the data until the lowest error is found. An ML algorithm guarantees that if we provide data in a particular format with some metric related to its output, it will generate some mathematical transformation that reveals the optimal value of the metric we offered. ML isn't an artificial intelligence. It is just algorithms that perform math on the numbers we feed in. ML does not comprehend the meaning of those numbers (it does not even know what, e.g., a date is). The only goal an ML algorithm has is to find an optimal value of a given evaluation metric while not knowing or caring about why it's optimizing that particular metric. So why all the hype about AI anyway? Let us have a look at one specific ML framework in more detail, notably Deep Learning (DL):

Deep Learning (DL) is a subset of ML, which some people describe as the next evolution of ML. DL algorithms are roughly inspired by how the human brain triggers neurons but far away from anything close to what the human brain is made of. Remember our CNN example app? It was very impressive indeed, but it was optimized for solving one very specific task. We can only use this model for predicting sketches, nothing else.

Whenever a machine completes tasks based on a set of stipulated rules that solve problems (algorithms), such an **"intelligent"** behavior is often called AI. I would wait to do that since I would still call it what it is, to call it by name: ML or DL. But of course, if we think of great vocal assistants like Google's Assistant or Amazon's Alexa, the results are already awe-inspiring. Let's consider all that immense hardware background and the scalability of these extensive data-trained systems. It is only fair enough for the proud engineers to call their babies AI, not only ML/DL.

There are endless discussions ongoing about what AI means. If it is highly overhyped or dangerously underestimated, but since that is not relevant for our sales analysis, it is just outside our remit. There are dozens of great resources if you want to demystify AI. I want to highlight one free MOOC in particular, which is from Finland`s University of Helsinki, since I greatly appreciate the democratized knowledge sharing in an easy-to-understand manner, where everyone is highly welcome to join this community:

https://www.elementsofai.com/

Hopefully, this will always be humankind`s aim: freely sharing knowledge for an even better world (even if this may sound too much like a cheap hipster slogan from Silicon Valley, I believe the core meaning is still a desirable approach)!

1.3.1 DATA SCIENCE

The ability to take data- to be able to understand it, to process it, to extract value from it, to visualize it, to communicate it – that's going to be a hugely important skill (Hal Varian, Google's Chief Economist, NYT, 2009).

When we use any of these three disciplines (ML, DL, or AI) for data analysis, can we already call it data science? A look at Drew Conway`s Venn diagram:

http://drewconway.com/zia/2013/3/26/the-data-science-venn-diagram

This Venn diagram helps us understand how Data Science fits into these concepts.

We can see at a glance that DS is not just only using ML, but it is the interface between ML, Traditional Research and the so-called "Danger Zone". DS deals with the analysis of data to extract knowledge, trying to solve real (business) problems by encompassing the coding, math, and domain knowledge subjects. Wikipedia describes DS as "a multidisciplinary field that uses scientific methods, processes, algorithms, and systems to extract knowledge and insights from structured and unstructured data." Besides possibly participating in tool building, a Data Scientist with substantive expertise would be the person who can run deep analyses on the data.

It is a fascinating interdisciplinary subject, encompassing everything from coding/math/statistics to domain knowledge to visualization/storytelling. Let us discuss these three areas more granularly.

Hacking Skills: why do we need to code at all? Could we not just use Excel and a BI tool like QlikSense? The first advantage of programming is reproducibility. When we write code instead of using point-and-click software, we can re-run it whenever our data changes, whether every day or year. The second advantage is flexibility. If QlikSense doesn't have a specific type of graph available, we won't be able to use it. But with programming, we can write our code. Even if we do not have the talent/time to write this code independently, we can still use Python`s community contribution (which is an excellent approach). Thousands of people create packages or code and publish them openly on GitHub or Pip (see chapter 1.7.3). We can use their code and amend it for our purpose. We're not reliant on a company if we know how to code. Just like the old saying: Give a man a fish, and we feed him for a day. Teach a man to fish, and we feed him for a lifetime.

Hacking skills for DS include both math and statistics. Both are mandatory. Otherwise, we will not understand our, e.g., matrix factorization or statsmodels during our coding part.

Domain knowledge: Since we run analyses on sales data, bookkeeping, and controlling, we can ask our sales force colleagues for any expert background. Expertise in data background knowledge is essential for understanding our data. Besides domain knowledge, we must also be strongly tied to different types of stakeholders. DS gathers expertise and insights by actively scanning trends/ best practices and provides them to our company. This means we must have an open ear for our colleagues who are not conducting analyses daily like us and, therefore, do not necessarily know by heart what, e.g., an overfitted model means. We constantly need to give feedback to our colleagues about whether our analyses are used and understood and if appropriate countermeasures are undertaken because only a living report is profitable for our company.

We have defined **machine learning** (ML) in chapter 1.1.2. If anything, we can state in this context that ML is not the most critical aspect of a DS's daily tasks (even if it might be to us, if we have more of an analyst background), but it is really a mixture of the three sectors hacking, domain knowledge, and ML.

The overlapping part between coding and domain knowledge, which DS does not cover, is called the "**danger zone**": data science practitioners lacking math or statistical knowledge can misapply techniques and draw false conclusions. Python sometimes throws an error at us when we code incorrectly. But more critical is when we receive results even though we have coded wrongly (applying the wrong logic). That's why we always need to cross-check our code and results critically.

Traditional research is the reason for **science** in DS.

Data scientists "tend to be "hard scientists", particularly physicists, rather than computer science majors. Physicists have a strong mathematical background, computing skills, and come from a discipline in which survival depends on getting the most from the data. They have to think about the big picture, the big problem" (DJ Patil, Chief Scientist at LinkedIn).

I believe that only a limited number of people analyze data using scientific means, but they still call themselves data scientists anyway. I am not a data scientist. This book runs machine learning models, but I would not call this data science. Even though we are not only using basic statistics for our sales analysis, we are still not using any scientific approaches. The only link between our sales analysis and science is that we use Python libraries, which are sometimes coded by scientists (who of you had ScikitLearn in mind first?). But why are we discussing all this DS background if we are seemingly not dealing with it? Many people would describe our approach as DS, maybe because they do not know any better or because DS sounds like a better sales pitch. At least we make sure that we understand the differences!

The good news is that even if not every one of us is a physicist, we can all try to think out of the box and sharpen our five analytic skills:

- Domain knowledge: knowing our data is key
- Statistics: without statistics, no ML
- Data wrangling: we have to roll up our sleeves
- ML: coding means mastering
- Tangibility: interactive storytelling helps, if we want to reach a broader audience

Our requester often wants an analysis done, not asking for anything like a scientific paper, but a best practice solution for this task. A core skill in DS is knowing how to translate a business situation into a data question, find the data answer, and deliver the business answer. If, for instance, our boss asks us for next week's sales results, we will not find any Python package called "next week's sales." But we must know how to use Facebook's Prophet for that task, e.g., We also need to know where the required data is stored and in what granularity. If we do not see, we cannot even tell how much our company sold yesterday.

Our goal of using deep analysis is also about building **data products**, not only answering questions like a data analyst. One example of a data product would be the interactive **visualizations** of our market basket analysis, which we will conduct in chapter 2. This graph network visualization should help us communicate our message and empower our report recipients to use the data on their own.

As with AI, we will only go into a little detail defining what DS is. However, we will concentrate on the pragmatic approach of DS. It is interesting for us to be aware of all these similar but different job titles that are often used interchangeably (identical to how AI, ML, DL, and DS usually get mixed up). Since data scientists work in an interdisciplinary manner, their duties will likely be mismatched to other job descriptions. What distinguishes a data scientist from a **Business Intelligence**, **Data Analyst**, **Data Engineer**, and **Statistician**?

Business Intelligence (BI) systems are strongly associated with a data warehouse, dashboards, or reports that consume data from the data warehouse and are used to answer particular questions. Data scientists are more bound to code that does open-ended analysis rather than produces a predefined output. Data Products from a DS are often not too adaptable when requirements change. Usually, BI is also more of a kind of service provider. Usually, they are not expected to consume their data products, perform their analysis, and make business decisions themselves. A data scientist instead would do. Data scientists may use data warehouses but also work with various less structured sources. In short, a DS will always be able to do a good BI job (since DS also covers BI, just in a broader sense). The other way around is not so easy.

If we are used to **databases**, we may not be familiar with unstructured data. So database guys bring many skills to the table to make them appropriate for data science tasks. But there's a focus on a particular data model, which is usually the relational data model (rows and columns). Having data from video/audio/text/graph sources, a relational database may or may not be the right tool. And even the concepts that transcend any particular database system may or may not be appropriate. We will not deal with unstructured data during our coding exercises, so let's move more to the analytic perspective.

If we are **business analysts**, we need to learn about algorithms and tradeoffs at scale. An analyst takes data and puts it in front of the right people. Usually, they work like an analyst, but they use less statistical and programming expertise. Their tool of choice is probably Power BI/Microstrategy/QlikView/ Tableau, etc, instead of Python, and they may never make statistical models. Although their job function is similar to that of an analyst, they create less sophisticated output because of the limitations of their tools and techniques. One example of their duties might be putting budget plans in a dashboard so management can track weekly progress. We could also build drill-downs that allow managers to quickly break down the plan numbers by country or product type. This work involves a lot of data cleaning and preparation but generally less work to interpret the data. Although we should be able to spot and fix data quality issues, the business partner is the primary person who makes decisions with this data. Thus, the job of an analyst is to take data from within the company, format and arrange it effectively, and deliver that data to others. However, much of the work, such as devising meaningful visualizations and deciding on particular data transformations, requires the same skills used in other cases. An analyst might be given a task such as "Create an automated dashboard that shows how our number of SalesItems is changing over time and grouped by customers." The analyst would have to find the appropriate data within the company, figure out how to transform the data appropriately, and then create a meaningful set of visually compelling dashboards and automatically update each day without errors. If we are **statisticians,** we need to learn to deal with data that usually does not fit into memory (RAM). We must learn to speak the business language of our colleagues and stakeholders (who are often not experts regarding topics like Triple exponential smoothing). Statistical methods are at the heart of any analyzing job. Still, statisticians are typically comfortable assuming that any data set they encounter will fit in the main memory of a single machine. However, a data scientist moves away from the past statistician's poor data to a data-rich regime, where the challenge is less on finding new mathematics to squeeze information out of a dataset than way more on new engineering even to handle or process massive datasets.

A **Data Engineer** develops, constructs, tests, and maintains architectures neatly stored and formatted in well-structured databases (DB) and large-scale processing systems, focusing on keeping data maintained in databases. Focusing more on the backend, a data engineer doesn't run reports, make analyses, or develop models. A data engineer may be tasked with maintaining all the customer records in a large-scale cloud database and adding new tables to that database as requested. Data engineers are said to be even more rare and in demand than data scientists. A data engineer updates the data processing flow when the jobs take too long. Other data engineers develop and monitor batch and streaming environments, managing data from collection to processing to storage. Data Engineers usually develop the core infrastructure, while DS is software-intensive, and data scientists create data products.

Summary:

In the past, receiving data was often complex, but nowadays, we are nearly drowning in data, e.g., your Twitter account. Today, **analytics** has replaced data acquisition as the bottleneck to evidence-based decision-making. Extracting knowledge from large, heterogeneous, and noisy datasets requires powerful computing resources and programming abstractions to use them effectively. Roughly speaking, a data scientist works on the data provided by a data engineer. So, the data engineer`s job would be to collect, move, or store the data. To collect the data, the engineer needs infrastructure to fetch this raw data and build reliable data flows. Only after that can the data scientists or analysts explore the data, evaluate it, and optimize the model. In the past, only a few people were skilled enough to do DS. However, since the frameworks are becoming increasingly well-known, the borders are steadily blurring.

1.4 STORY TELLING

Data scientists need to find not only nuggets of truth in data but explain it to the business leaders (Richard Snee, EMC).

Nailing future values precisely alone is not enough. In order to be effective, we need to explain and interpret our results and communicate findings accurately to stakeholders to inform business decisions. Visualization is the field of research in computer science that studies effective communication of quantitative results.

In chapter 2, we will conduct our analysis step by step using interactive visualizations. Regarding sharing our insights with our colleagues, there are many possible solutions to this task. We could directly share our Python script as a Jupyter Notebook. This is handy if our colleagues are already familiar with (or at least not afraid of) Python.

But assuming our colleagues are not coders or statisticians, let's say we are analyzing for our salesforce colleagues: our sales colleagues probably prefer an easy-to-understand but also performant, user-friendly, and visually eye-catching report (doesn't that dashboard look sexy?). If our company already has BI tools (Tableau, Power BI, QlikView, Microstrategy, Cognos ..) in use, that would be a very sensible bridge between our ML model results and the department we are doing it all for.

In chapter 2, we will transform from our Jupyter Notebook to a data product. I could have written a complete book about data visualization (storytelling), but luckily, other people are much more blessed with this essential skill. For instance, have a look at these experts` wonderful and aspiring work:

https://www.visualcinnamon.com/

https://www.nytimes.com/by/mike-bostock

http://elijahmeeks.com/

1.5 AI WINTER
VS AI HYPE

Instead of summing up the previous chapter about ML, AI, and DS, let us instead compare reality vs hype, having a look at current examples, like forecasting stock prices:

Would it not be awesome to have an **ML symposium** at our fingertips to forecast future stock price development? Of course, it would, and many people work hard to predict stock prices as accurately as possible. But even today, with all this big data available, no one has yet achieved this goal sustainably. Even though dozens of features are available that influence stock prices, no model can fit all these features to our target, which is the stock price. The reason is that the influences are too complex and often changing. Too noisy, in one word. Until now, no model has been able to forecast stock prices correctly in the long run. Too many unpredictable events happen all the time, and no model can digest the patterns behind them early enough. In 2018, who would have considered an upcoming pandemic with a substantial economic impact called COVID-19? Who would have thought that an American president declared Bavarian cars a national security threat? There are lots and lots of examples to list. Still, we got the point: all these happenings influence the stock market (even if sometimes more due to human psychology rather than rationality), so predicting future stock prices will continue meaning to read tea leaves and human gut feeling (okay, to be fair plus expertise knowledge and tremendous data support). But as long as we lack automatic extracting knowledge from data on a global scale, the enormous demand for human expert data analysts will remain high for bringing all the relevant patterns together in one fruitful strike.

But what about Blackrock, the world-famous American investment management corporation? They are said to make great use of automatic data decisions thanks to mass data (big data) processing and many advanced ML models. That is true, and this powerfully demonstrates what already makes ML so impressive today. Blackrock has vast amounts of data available to rank their choices. Even though this is not a self-learning artificial intelligence, it generates insights out of the box (out of the scope it was initially trained on) and decides about measures to take. However, automated data mining on big data, with the help of machine learning algorithms, generates scalable answers and is already influencing the company's choices. It would be impossible for humans to oversee this vast amount of data at scale and make decisions on it. This already proves what ML can do nowadays. The models will certainly be trained constantly in the future. These models will gain more predictive power with persistently evolving hardware and algorithms. It is up to us to further broaden our ML skills and control that our **ethical standards** don`t get a raw deal (see chapter 1.6.3).

Today, we face ML models in so many applications that we hardly recognize them anymore. Regarding our task of trying to cluster and forecast sales, there is a famous example from the US supermarket chain Walmart: Walmart analyzed their big sales data to surprisingly find out that before announced hurricanes, customers not only stock up with water, batteries, and torches but also with strawberry pop tarts and beer. Even some people now might argue that it is just common sense to fill up your beer stock before any hurricane, it was very surprising even to Walmart that pop tarts with natural strawberry filling sell seven times more shortly before hurricanes, compared to nonhurricane season (ML shows **correlation,** not the **causation** behind). It would have been nearly impossible for humans to find this particular pattern in this mass of data.

In summary, generally predicting data mostly means **fitting models** with data. And that is a crucial point: we should always fit a model to the data! We should not fit the data into the model since we are trying to gather knowledge from our data. We achieve this using ML, which AI is just the overhead of (in case we orchestrate our ML Symposium). We need to receive the data (data engineer) and process/analyze it meaningfully (data scientist/ analyst). The machine is much better at optimizing than humans, but formulation and evaluation are still up to us. Because AI/ML can't be creative like humans, it cannot see the big picture and bring it all together. This is one of the most outstanding reasons I find ML so extremely thrilling: right now, people have achieved so much in the field of ML (cancer image classification, natural language processing, etc), but there is still so much to pioneer. We are still early enough to join the exciting ML community. Let us ultimately start our Python engine to set up our ML models.

1.6 TECHNICAL SET UP

What setup is necessary to build statistical and ML models to help us predict future values or spot unseen patterns? **Python** can do that job more than sufficiently. If not already the case, we will now install Python and Packages as a basic premise to be able to run our Python code in chapter 2.

1.6.1 JUPYTER NOTEBOOKS

Python is a coding language that is not explicitly bound to specific duties. Python is highly appreciated in scientific data processing and for tasks in DS and ML. For Python developing projects, it is a good approach to use Jupyter Notebooks. IPython is closely tied with the Jupyter project (https://jupyter.org/), which provides a browser-based valuable notebook for development, collaboration, and sharing. In Jupyter Notebooks, we can execute Python statements interactively cell by cell, plot static and dynamic visualizations, collaborate with our colleagues transparently and conveniently, add screenshots into our code via markup, and add some nice formatting for better readability. Furthermore, these documents can be saved, and others can open and execute the code on their systems. By the way, this document was also written initially entirely within a Jupyter Notebook.

There are many different options for getting Python in our Jupyter Notebook started. For simplicity, I will explain it for one instance: using the Python distribution Anaconda, which is a perfect choice for both beginners and experienced Python coders.

The reason for coding Python within Jupyter Notebook is they're both free and open source, meaning that many people, not just one company or one group, contribute code that we can use. They have many packages (sets of code) for data wrangling and machine learning from which to choose. Of course, we could also use R, Matlab, etc., to train ML models. There are endless discussions about the pros and cons of Python vs R, but we will not join them here. We chose Python because it is an excellent language for ML and coding, and a vast community is behind it. Please trust me; we will not regret choosing Python (and yes, R is also fantastic, but just not as awesome as Python:-)).

The reason for choosing **Anaconda** (besides the fact that Anaconda and Python make sense from a species point of view:-)) is the world's most popular Python distribution platform, with over 20 million users worldwide (according to Anaconda). Besides convenience, we do this because we trust Anaconda`s long-term commitment to supporting this open-source ecosystem. Anaconda is a Python Distribution for Windows, Linux, and MacOS existing out of Ipython (Python Command Line), Spyder (Editor for Python), Jupyter Notebooks (editor in our browser which can also contain formatted texts and images, besides Python code) and conda (**package management system**). We do not need to worry too much about these tools, except for Jupyter Notebook, Conda, and Ipython.

Ipython is Python's shell, which offers more functionality than the basic Python prompt. If you want more details, you can also check Anaconda's website, which is optional for conducting our sales analysis in chapter 2. All we need to know for our sales analysis task is how to install Anaconda to get Jupyter Notebook running and how to import new libraries.

To install Python via Anaconda, please go to:

https://www.anaconda.com/products/individual

Click the download button to decide which Python version you want to download. I recommend to use the most current version available, which currently would be Python 3.11. Only install Python 2 if you know why you would do that. You will prevent yourself from unnecessary versioning troubleshooting if you stick to the newest (stable) available Python version right from the start.

The downloading wizard will take you through all the steps. You can stick to the default destination folder as suggested by Anaconda:

Destination Folder

C:\Users\jesko\anaconda3   Browse...

Space required: 3.0GB

In this example, C:\Users\jesko is also the folder where we will pip install any Python packages to (see next chapter).

It is recommended that you register Anaconda as your primary Python. Please also stick to this default setting unless you know why you would like to add it to your path environment:

Advanced Options

☐ Add Anaconda3 to my PATH environment variable

Not recommended. Instead, open Anaconda3 with the Windows Start menu and select "Anaconda (64-bit)". This "add to PATH" option makes Anaconda get found before previously installed software, but may cause problems requiring you to uninstall and reinstall Anaconda.

☑ Register Anaconda3 as my default Python 3.7

This will allow other programs, such as Python Tools for Visual Studio PyCharm, Wing IDE, PyDev, and MSI binary packages, to automatically detect Anaconda as the primary Python 3.7 on the system.

After your installation has finished, we can start our Jupyter Notebook. Though the Jupyter Notebook is viewed and edited through our web browser window, it must connect to a Python running process to execute code. This process is known as a "kernel" and can be started using two different approaches:

either starting from your programs:

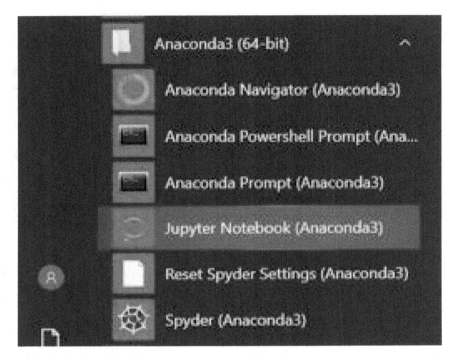

Or directly out of your Anaconda Prompt, run the following command in your system **shell** (Anaconda prompt): jupyter notebook

And that is what Jupyter Notebook will look like after starting in your browser:

What happened is that a local web server has been launched that is visible to your browser. It immediately spits out a log showing

what it is doing:

Usually, the browser should open automatically, but in case it does not, we can also just enter http://localhost:8888 (default setting).

The Jupyter Notebook is a browser-based graphical interface to the Python shell, including interactive display capabilities. Thanks to its easy syntax, Python is a beginner-friendly language. Unlike other languages that require specific uses of curly brackets and semicolons, Python only cares about **indentation.** This is important to remember because Python will not be able to debug if the ident is not set correctly.

To create a new Jupyter Notebook click on the "New" button and select "Python 3":

In your new notebook, to give your project a name double-click on the "Untitled" header:

And call it whatever you like:

The most important thing to know about Jupyter Notebook for a beginner is the cell, in which you enter all your Python code:

After entering your Python code in your cell, you can execute the code by clicking on the "Run" button (or use Shift+Enter while the cell you want to execute is activated).

Use markup language to add headers and screenshots to your project. When finished, click the "Save" button to close your project. You will be able to find your project on your Jupyter Notebook start page, and you can open any projects from there by simply clicking on it:

After typing the name of a variable, object, or function following the. character hit the "Tab" key. Typing "Tab" brings up a list of available options. Scroll through the list or type a letter to filter the list to certain starting letters. Use "Enter" to select the option you want.

Tab completion can also be used during module import. Hit "Tab" after typing the module name to see which functions and classes are available in that module.

from pandas import <tab>

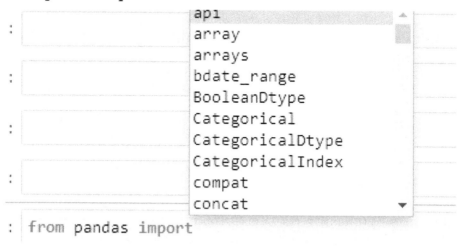

After importing a module, you can use the help() function to see documentation about the command if it is available.

You can also call the help () function to see documentation about the command if it is available:

```
In [7]: help(list)

Help on class list in module builtins:

class list(object)
 |  list(iterable=(), /)
 |
 |  Built-in mutable sequence.
 |
 |  If no argument is given, the constructor creates a new empty list.
 |  The argument must be an iterable if specified.
 |
 |  Methods defined here:
 |
 |  __add__(self, value, /)
 |      Return self+value.
 |
 |  __contains__(self, key, /)
 |      Return key in self.
 |
 |  __delitem__(self, key, /)
```

1.6.2 LIBRARIES

Anaconda already comes with a variety of **libraries** pre-installed:

These libraries (packages) are the core of our ML heart. However, we will install many other libraries during our analyst career. Before going into detail, let us first define why libraries are helpful. Libraries will make our life so much easier, because they will bring us both performance and broader functionality without the need of core coding by ourselves. When talking about ML, we mostly talk about the algorithms used in specific libraries. Prophet, for instance, is one library owned by Meta (formerly known as Facebook), which we will use to predict sales in chapter 2.3.2.

Any new library can be installed using "**pip install**" in the Anaconda prompt.

If you want to pip install, go to and search for your desired package:

https://pypi.org/project/ (Python Package Index)

For instance, if you want to pip install opencv, that would be your link: https://pypi.org/project/opencv-python/

There, you will find the pip code snippet, which you can copy and paste into the Anaconda prompt:

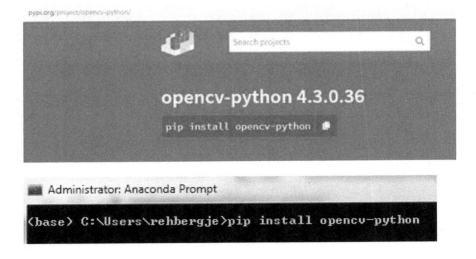

The great thing about installing per pip is that pip will take care of any coherences between your installed packages. So if you want to install package a, and that package is dependent on package b, you will be asked also to install package b automatically.

If we need to upgrade a specific library- let's say we want to upgrade our existing scikit-learn library to version 0.21.3- we can enter the following command in our anaconda prompt:

conda install scikit-learn=0.21.3

We could now go on and pip install all python packages we will need. But there is one important point: packages can have concurrences, which could cause trouble. So it could be that you have already installed some packages We could now pip install all the Python packages we will need. However, there is one crucial point: packages can have concurrences, which could cause trouble. You could have already installed some packages, and everything worked well. Now that you are adding a new package via the usual **pip install**, some old packages do not work any longer. That's the reason why it is best practice to use **virtual environments**. My preferred way of doing this is using a **YAML** file. The YAML file combines the pros of using a virtual environment (venv) plus adding better maintainability (having the complete overview of packages used in one file). Below is the environment for the RFM analysis that we will use in a later chapter:

```
name: env_rfm
channels:
  - conda-forge
  - fastai
  - pytorch
  - plotly
  - gcc
dependencies:
  - python>=3.6
#  - python=3.5
  - pandas
  - ipython
  - numpy
  - pyodbc
  - jupyter
#  - apyori
  - matplotlib
  - mlxtend
  - seaborn
  - plotly
  - plotly_express==0.4.0
  - xlrd >= 1.0.0
  - openpyxl
  - fbprophet
  - scikit-learn
  - tensorflow
  - pyspark
```

To activate such an environment via yaml file, first we have to create the name in conda:

conda create --name env_rfm python=3.7 -y

Then we create the environment:

conda env create -f environment.yml

After we have created the environment we can now activate it:

conda activate env_rfm

to finally being able to start Jupyter Notebook by entering in your conda:

Jupyter Notebook

In case we want to change or refresh our environment we have to use update in conda:

conda env update -f "Desktop\environment.yml"

You can find the complete YAML file for the RFM coding chapter in my Github repository:

https://github.com/DAR-DatenanalyseRehberg

As soon as we have imported the necessary **packages** for our report purposes, we can simply import these modules into our Jupyter Notebook, e.g.:

```
import pandas as pd
```

Afterward, we can run all Pandas functions by calling pd.functionname. It's good practice to place all necessary imports right at the beginning of your script for a better overview. In any case, it's essential to place the import before you call the function. Many modules are conditional on other modules, but luckily, we do not need to worry since Python will ensure that no module is imported twice.
In case you should be puzzled about the difference between packages and modules, let's state this more clearly using this example (see also chapter 2.4.1):

```
import matplotlib.pyplot as plt
```

Matplotlib is the package, while Pyplot is the module. Packages have the convenient advantage of storing some modules in one package.
As a last note, we can also use "from..import", like we do for mounting the Google Drive (see chapter 2):

```
from google.colab import drive
drive.mount('/content/gdrive')
```

This means we only import the function "drive" from the Colab module, and we can call the function name without mentioning the module name before.

Even though we can run the sales analysis locally, sometimes we won't be able to train a model with our **local hardware** (training might break or take hours), which brings us to the next chapter.

1.6.3 CLOUD PLATFORMS

As already mentioned, fitting models quite often demands serious computational resources. So, using **Cloud's** power is not a question of if but when.

Note: no matter what Cloud vendor you choose, please always make sure that uploading data into a cloud is aligned with your company's IT principles beforehand. Always make sure that you are allowed to use the data you want to analyze and only keep it stored, computed, analyzed, and visualized in a safe and regulated (if needed) environment, whatever that means, in particular in your company.

First of all, I recommend checking out Google's **Colab.** It's not a cloud platform but a free Jupyter Notebook environment that runs completely in the cloud without any setup required. It is an extremely helpful and convenient way to run, save, and share (Colab is short for Colaboratory) our analysis in our browser. On top of that "sharing is caring" idea, we also receive a Tesla **GPU** for free (or **TPU**). GPU stands for graphics Processing Units and is very supportive of, for example, Tensorflow, an extremely popular library we will discuss in more detail later.

To check Colab out please go to:

https://colab.research.google.com/

Only when you're signed in with your Google account will you be able to save your Jupyter Notebooks and files to your Google

Drive? The rest is similar to your local Jupyter Notebook. You only need to know how to import data files from your Google Drive into your Google Colab Jupyter Notebook.

```
from google.colab import drive
drive.mount('/content/gdrive')
```

Afterward, click on the link and use and copy the token directly into your Jupyter Notebook.

Colab will now let you know that you are mounted at /content/gdrive, so you can import your data file like this if you have uploaded your data into Google's drive beforehand (into the DDDD-Folder):

```
import pandas as pd
data = pd.read_excel('/content/gdrive/My Drive/DDDDFolder/DDDD.xlsx')
data.head()
```

As an alternative, you can also upload files directly using this cell:

```
import pandas as pd

from google.colab import files

files.upload()

df = pd.read_excel("DDDD.xlsx")
```

Colab comes with many packages already pre-installed. Only sometimes will you need to explicitly pip install these (see chapter 1.6.3). The rest of Colab looks and behaves quite similar to your local Jupyter Notebook, only running in the cloud. My advice to you is to run this book`s code in Colab first. This way, you will make sure that everything will work perfectly fine. Afterward, you can adapt the code to your data needs in your local Jupyter Notebook environment.

While Colab is a Cloud solution only for Jupyter Notebooks, let us now shortly check the giant cloud platforms (which cover all your data needs, not only the Jupyter Notebook itself):

Google Cloud Platform (GCP):

https://cloud.google.com/

Google offers unique APIs to its products, so we can build an app that makes something like this possible: Take a photo of a street sign in a foreign language, and Google will translate it into your language. Google is a massive player in ML speech recognition, video, and picture classification. For instance, setting up a Chatbot (Dialog Flow) that connects with your Google calendar is easy, so the Chatbot can automatically arrange meetings for you. We can expect that using Google libraries like Tensorflow on GCP is made as easy as possible, with lots of well-written and supportive tutorials by Google.

Amazon Web Service (AWS):

https://aws.amazon.com/

AWS: Amazon is a worldwide cloud leader and famous for its ML know-how. So, I can repeat pretty much all of what I've said about GCP. Worth mentioning is Amazon's Mechanical Turk, which we discuss later in this chapter.

Microsoft Azure:

https://azure.microsoft.com/

Using Azure might be very interesting if you are strongly tied to Microsoft's Office products (even though this is not the only reason for going with Azure). So, if you already work with Power BI, Access, Excel, Outlook, and SQL Server, these programs are nicely integrated within Azure.

IBM Watson Studio:

https://www.ibm.com/cloud/ai

IBM's Watson Studio is also a serious player in ML, even though the ML community seems more attracted to AWS, Google, and Microsoft. Similar to what we just said about Azure, it also counts for Watson: if you already use a lot of IBM programs, choosing Watson might make a lot of sense.

Alibaba:

https://eu.alibabacloud.com/

Does the USA rule the cloud platform market? Well, at least there is also Alibaba from China, even though they might not yet have the same market share, at least in Europe.

The big five cloud platforms can do the job as soon as we get used to them. But there are still some topics we need to keep in mind:

Using ML as a Service (**MLaaS**) means trusting these companies to build general-purpose ML algorithms. The big players take care of the data collection, training, and model deployment to interpret our data (of course, we have to pay for this service in exchange). Unfortunately, when using an MLaaS solution, we have no control over how the model is built. Collecting data, training a model, and setting up the infrastructure is the vendor's job, which is very comfortable for us. We only have to integrate their solution into our data product. Thanks to MLaaS, we have become much quicker in prototyping. However, that "laziness" comes with a price tag: we depend on the vendor since we don't own the underlying technology. We must trust them in their ongoing support, security, and privacy. And that might or might not be okay with your company's principles.

Instead of using an MLaaS solution, we could choose to use only an **ML platform product**. Here, we would upload our own training data to optimize a ready-to-use model for our specific needs. There is one famous example of a cucumber classification task where the advantage of Google's image classification models has been used and fine-tuned with a labeled dataset of cucumbers: https://cloud.google.com/blog/products/gcp/how-a-japanese-cucumber-farmer-is-using-deep-learning-and-tensorflow

ML platforms use **transfer learning**'s strengths (standing on the shoulders of giants) to allow customers like us to use the provider's expertise in modeling while adapting to niche needs like the cucumber classification example. The ML platform's model is hosted in the provider's cloud (similar to MLaaS), and we just submit requests.

We should be aware that when we decide on a specific cloud vendor, they will try to bind us to their services sustainably (at least, from their perspective). These cloud vendors are revenue-triggered. I do not want to give us the creeps at all. Of course, making money with one's service is legitimate and necessary. What I want to stress is that until now, we have talked about Python and Python Packages, which are all free/ open source, like Google's TensorFlow, Uber's Ludwig, Facebook's Prophet, Pytorch, Airbnb's Airflow, Spotify's Luigi, Apple's Turicreate, ING's Sparse_Dot_Topn, etc. On the cloud platforms, we will use many vendor-specific tools (Big Query, etc). In our process, cloud computation power may come at a cost, such as data protection, vendor binding, and "hard to know before costs" (service on demand). If using MLaaS should not be an option for you, you would have to go the "hard" way. By building your model in your environment, you gain complete flexibility and control over your technology, data, and modelThe reason why I am mentioning this? Do we want to use open source, where our personal skill set is the most limiting factor? Or do we prefer the easier way: getting good results in a shorter time without necessarily understanding all the steps in between? At least, we only need to take care of some of the primary data engineering tasks when deciding on one of these cloud vendors. Using open algorithms requires skills and, hopefully, long-lasting community support, but it puts more self-dependent power in our hands. However, that comfort comes with the cost of depending on the big ones (Alibaba, Amazon, Google, etc.). That's just the way it is. Indeed, there is competition for the big players as well. To name only one upcoming from Europe, Gaia X might become an attractive alternative that could better comply with your business compliance rules.

But enough of my German Angst: compare the pros and cons for your specific needs and then enjoy the opportunities these solutions will bring..

Let us keep our human touch a little further more, and get even more social: it is still the human helping the machines to learn!

Let us keep our human touch a little further and get even more social: it is still humans helping machines learn!

Let's say you're a sheep farmer and you are building a spring gun, which should automatically shoot the wolf, but neither the sheepdog nor the sheep (okay, I admit that might not be the most friendly example I could have come up with, but hey, I am just human). The model should correctly separate between dogs/sheep and wolves. If unclear, the model must be classified as not a wolf by default. We must feed in many wolf and dog/sheep images to train that model and label them all correctly. If we do not want to label our data by ourselves, we can also use, eg. Google's labeling service:

https://cloud.google.com/ai-platform/data-labeling/docs?hl=de

But will our data be correctly labeled and handled according to GDPA, and will the anonymous human worker get paid according to **social standards** (if yes, standards of which country)? Well, one way to find out is to apply for exactly that job on Amazon's Mechanical Turk

https://www.mturk.com/

Mechanical Turk is a platform that brings both sides together: people who need support labeling their data by humans (often as a kick-start during the early modeling phase) and people who are willing to help (the mechanic Turks behind the machine, so to speak). This is a fascinating platform. You will probably not become rich working as a mechanical Turk, but it is very motivating to support the ML community to the next level.

I am seriously mentioning this because, in ML, we will often face the challenge of labeling lots of data (not to speak of big data here) during the start phase. There is generally also the chance of using Pretrained Models as a temporary help. This can only help if your data is not too unique (otherwise, you won't find any models trained on similar data). "Standing on the shoulders of giants" means something in this context. This can be supportive, but remember that we are unaware of the model's background. For instance, there is this famous example from Google, which was primarily trained with images of white people. So, the model misclassified a black person as a gorilla:

https://www.theverge.com/2018/1/12/16882408/google-racist-gorillas-photo-recognition-algorithm-ai

We must discuss **bias** in machine learning models (some models might be imbalanced, e.g., between different genders, races, socio-economic backgrounds, etc.). Just think of models used by the police or judges to estimate people`s probability of specific criminal activity. In these cases, it is crystal clear that the correct training, validation, and testing of the model is mandatory and deserves the highest public focus and permanent surveillance. Last, the question is whether data is critical to all questions. With regards to house prices, data is undoubtedly very supportive, but can available data really tell if someone is innocent or not?

1.7 WISDOM OF CROWDS

From the last chapter`s human touch, we will now move to **knowledge-sharing platforms** where we can use the wisdom of crowds (Schwarmintelligenz is the beautiful German word for it). We will not discuss freelancer platforms where you can hire people to work through your analysis projects. However, we are more interested in getting to know the platforms where we can find answers to our questions, like Kaggle, Stackoverflow, and Github. All three of them are a great source of inspiration and knowledge sharing.

1.7.1 KAGGLE

Kaggle is a great online community platform owned by Google for DS and ML competitions. Besides the fact that we will find hundreds of thousands of inspirational **projects** and **datasets,** the interesting part is that we can also use Kaggle to run our code in a web-based environment (similar to what Google Colab is offering). If you want to download datasets from Kaggle or wish to run scripts directly on Kaggle, you need to set up an account first:

https://www.kaggle.com/

1.7.2
STACKOVERFLOW

As soon as we run into errors in our Jupyter Notebook project which we cannot solve on our own, Stack Overflow is a great platform to get our questions answered, share knowledge, and exchange with other coders:

https://stackoverflow.com/

For Data Scientists they even have a particular domain in place: https://datascience.stackexchange.com/

1.7.3 GITHUB

GitHub is a web-based hosting service that uses a Git **repository** and belongs to Microsoft. Git is a distributed software development version control system we can access through Github. Github (and Git) are both free and open-source software. Version control is a method of tracking how code changes over time. Version control lets us store our files, revert them to a previous time, and see who changed what file, how, and when. This mechanism is essential for data scientists working in teams (helping keep track of changes in code and collaboration) because if someone accidentally changes a file that breaks our code, we want the ability to revert or see what has changed. If two people are working on the same file separately, Git makes sure that no one's work is ever accidentally deleted or overwritten.

Even though Git is mainly meant for version control for coders, I believe that the most crucial aspect for us is to use it to get the code of other people via Github:

There are an incredible number of projects out there with astonishing levels of quality, and they are just waiting for us to be **cloned, pulled,** or **pushed** into the **repository.**

I personally believe there is no faster way to learn data analysis than seeing and understanding what other smart people have done and amending it so it works with your own data. Doing so will bring us the best results within the shortest time possible. So, if you don`t already have a Github account, I strongly encourage you to set one up right now.

Go to Github.com, create a new account, and you will be all set within a few minutes. Now, it's time to familiarize yourself with the most important Github functions for accessing other people's code.

https://github.com/DAR-DatenanalyseRehberg/

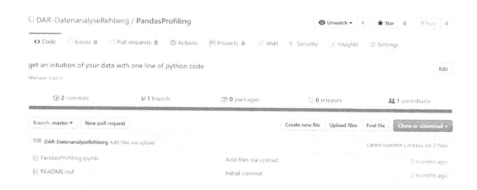

We can study the readme file to receive information about the project first. If we click "Clone or download," we can save the whole project locally on our PC.

Now that we understand the basic background behind ML Concepts, how to install Python and libraries, and where to get help, let's finally put all these theories into practice and start coding.

2. ANALYSIS

We will use Jupyter Notebook in Colab to run our Python sales analysis code. Please refer to chapter 1.6.3 to know how to access Colab. Colab gives us the advantage of not stressing too much about installing the necessary packages. Using Colab, I can ensure that the code below will run (something I cannot guarantee on your local machine because of all your possible specific package dependencies). However, you can also run this Jupyter Notebook on your PC (a virtual environment is best practice; see chapter 1.6.1) if you do not want to use Colab. No matter what path you prefer, I highly recommend running the code instead of only reading it: only those who code will truly understand.

You'll find all the Jupyter Notebook code in my Github repository:

https://github.com/DAR-DatenanalyseRehberg/DDDD_Data-Driven-Dealings-Development

As a general introduction to the coding part, let me explain the structure of this chapter in front:

Every coding chapter starts with theoretical but very coding-specific prose. Then, we will look at the Jupyter Notebook cells, which are the same as in my Github repository. Comments in the code are highlighted in green and always start with a "#". I recommend reading each coding cell first in this book and then running it on your own in your Jupyter Notebook. At least for me, that is the most fruitful approach to learning and understanding the code.

Before we can start the Jupyter Notebook in Colab, first of all, we have to upload the file DDDD.xlsx into Google Drive (I have created the folder DDDD-folder for this example):

(screenshot taken from Google's Drive)

Then we can switch to Google Colab:

https://colab.research.google.com/

And start a new Jupyter Notebook (or just the Jupyter Notebook, which you have forked from my Github repository before):

(screenshot taken from Google's Colab)

The very first code we have to enter in one Jupyter Notebook cell is about to mount our Google Drive in Colab, so we can import our data file into our Jupyter Notebook project to be able to work with that data afterward:

To be able to use your data stored in your Google Drive you first need to mount your Google Drive so you can load and save files to it.
from **google.colab** import **drive**
drive.mount('/content/gdrive')
#You'll need to put in a token which Google will generate for you as soon as you click on the link

After you have entered this code into your cell you can run it by pressing the "Run" button (or use the shortcut shift+enter):

+ Code   + Text

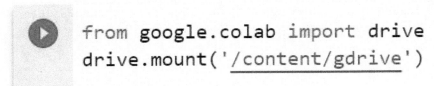

```
from google.colab import drive
drive.mount('/content/gdrive')
```

(screenshot taken from Google's Colab)

Afterwards, copy and paste your token, and you're ready to start:

Google

Anmeldung

Kopieren Sie diesen Code, wechseln Sie zu Ihrer Anwendung und geben Sie ihn dort ein:

4/4QGOeb9EaJwYw-
AX7bs6kzCQq58GlhHAq6TVnd9LyTjWxJrO6IjMPVE

Copy your token/code, paste it, and press enter:

```
Go to this URL in a browser: https://accounts.google.com/o

Enter your authorization code:
4/4QGOeb9EaJwYw-AX7bs6kzCQq58GlhHAq6TVnd9LyTjWxJrO6IjMPVE
```

If everything works correctly, you will receive this message:

Mounted at /content/gdrive

Using Pandas, we can import the Excel file into a data frame (df). Pandas is a well-known data analysis module that mainly deals with data frames. We will call our data frame "data":

```
import pandas as pd
data = pd.read_excel('/content/gdrive/My Drive/DDDDFolder/
DDDD.xlsx')
```

Hint:

Alternatively, you can also upload a file without uploading it into your Google Drive account first:

import pandas as pd

```
from google.colab import files
files.upload()
df = pd.read_excel("DDDD.xlsx")
```

In Python, we can store values in variables. Variables can be freely named before the "=". In our case, we store the Excel file in the variable df (which stands for dataframe). A data frame is the central data structure in Pandas, quite similar to a table in Excel. Technically, a data frame consists of a series of series, each describing a column. A series is a list of data with an index, so you can pick up a specific row using the index.

We access the Excel file DDDD using a Pandas function (for convenience, we use the alias pd, which is standard practice) called "read_excel". We can call this Excel import function because we imported the Panda's library, which includes this easy and convenient function for importing Excel files. We have to use the inverted comma "" in 'DDDD.xlsx' to tell Python that what stands in between the" is a string. We can add comments to our code anytime using the # sign.

Hint:

If we want to extract data directly out of our data warehouse, here is one example for a sql server connection:

```
import pandas as pd
import pyodbc
sql_conn = pyodbc.connect('Driver={SQL Server};'
            'Server=MsSqlServerName;'
            'Database=DatabaseName;'
            'Trusted_Connection=NO;UID=USER;PWD=PASS
WORD)
```

query = "SELECT * from dbo.DDDD "

df = pd.read_sql(query, sql_conn)

The Data file "DDDD.xlsx" includes sales data on the following granularity: the sales amount of items per sales date per customer and sales transaction ID. We can have a look at our df calling the head function any time:

data.head()

	SalesDate	SalesValue	SalesAmount	Customer	SalesTransactionID	SalesItem
0	2018-09-28	8280.0	10	0	0	0
1	2018-09-28	7452.0	10	0	0	0
2	2019-04-23	21114.0	30	0	1	0
3	2019-04-23	7038.0	10	0	1	1
4	2019-04-23	7000.0	2	0	1	2

A Df can be compared to an Excel table with indexed rows and columns.

Hint:

 # # Just in case your data needs a little bit of preparation, I have attached some very frequently used data massaging functions

 # # Let`s assume you want to rename the column header SalesValue into Net Sales and SalesTransactionID into Transaction, you can use the rename function:

 #   data=data.rename(columns={'SalesValue':   'Net   Sales', 'SalesTransactionID': 'Transaction'})

 # # If you want to concatenate two columns, separated by -&- you could do so like that:

 #   data["SalesItemCustomer"]   =   data["SalesItem"]   +'-&-'+

data["Customer"]

 # And in case you want to separate the column SalesItemCustomer again into two columns, -&- as the separator, use the split function with n =1, if you want to split into two columns:

 # new = data["SalesItemCustomer"].str.split("-&-", n = 1, expand = True)

 # # Making separate SalesItemSep column from new data frame:

 # data["SalesItemSep"]= new[0]

 # # Making separate CustomerSep column from new data frame:

 # data["CustomerSep"]= new[1]

If we keep our brackets empty (just like we did when stating head()), Pandas will, by default, display the first five rows. Please see that the first indexed row starts with a 0; therefore, the fifth row has the index counter 4. If we want to check, let's say, the first ten rows instead of five, we would do it like this:

data.head(10)

As we can see, the data regarding the number of features (Customer, SalesID, Sales Item) is minimal. Can we predict sales, run market basket analysis, and recommend items on these few features? Let's see!

We will extract insights from the data to understand our customer sales behavior in a better way (EDA and RFM, see chapter 2.1) and estimate future sales (predicting, see chapter 2.3). We will continually benchmark our prediction against actuals afterward, trying to determine where any possible deviation might come from (customer churn due to competition, higher discount to reach out to more sales, etc). That is the reason this book is called "Data Driven Dealings Development".

We want to understand past sales precisely and predict the future as accurately as possible. Also, we want to recommend our customers products that they should be interested in but have not yet purchased. We are also doing so to support our salesforce colleagues in treating our customers how they deserve (see KPI definition in chapter 1.2.3.2) and help them act proactively before they buy less or turn themselves to our competition. For the sake of higher precision, we will enrich our data (feature engineering, chapter 1.2.3.2), use unsupervised ML clustering (chapter 2.2), and use supervised ML techniques (chapter 2.3).

So, what we are going to do with the data is:

- Explore the data (EDA: exploratory data analysis)
- Analyse sales for Recency, Frequency and Monetary value (RFM) using unsupervised ML
- Predict future sales (while looking at past sales) using supervised ML
- Analyse market baskets (frequently bought together items) using the Apriori Package
- Recommend Products (recommend item x to customer y due to similar other customers purchases) using matrix factorization

When trying to predict future sales or recommend items, we do this based on data from the past. Ideally, our recommendations will build a bridge from past to future sales, when hopefully, our recommended items will lead to more future sales.

2.1 EDA

After we have imported the data into our data frame, we will have a more detailed look at the data. We will use descriptive statistics and visualize some (exploratory data analysis). First of all, we are going to analyze the shape and distribution of our data:

```
# As we can see from the above data.head we have six columns.
The len function would do the same for us.
print(len(data.columns))
# Just using len() on our dataframe will tell us the amount of
rows.
print(len(data))
#result: six columns in total where: a Customer buys a SalesItem
on a specific SalesDate. Depending on the SalesAmount
(Quantity the SalesItems is purchased) the SalesValue (e.g. in
€) will vary. Sometimes the customer buys more than one
SalesItem at once (in one SalesTransactionID).
#the corresponding features.
#Instead of using len two times we can also achieve the same
result using shape.
data.shape
# Check if there are any missing inputs (NaN stands for Not a
Number)
print(data.isnull().any(axis=1).sum(), ' / ', len(data))
# SalesDate looks like a Date data type, but let's make sure using
dtypes function.
print(data.dtypes)
```

```
SalesDate                datetime64[ns]
SalesValue                      float64
SalesAmount                       int64
Customer                          int64
SalesTransactionID                int64
SalesItem                         int64
dtype: object
```

SalesDate is Datetime as expected. But it may be uncommon for you to see that the customer is int (integer, instead of a customer name string (str)). The reason for using a whole number (int) is it is used as a primary key. We will see how to map it back to customer names later on.

#info() even adds information about non-null to the above used dtypes() function, so we do not need to use isnull separately.
data.info()

```
<class 'pandas.core.frame.DataFrame'>
RangeIndex: 341422 entries, 0 to 341421
Data columns (total 6 columns):
 #   Column              Non-Null Count   Dtype
---  ------              --------------   -----
 0   SalesDate           341422 non-null  datetime64[ns]
 1   SalesValue          341422 non-null  float64
 2   SalesAmount         341422 non-null  int64
 3   Customer            341422 non-null  int64
 4   SalesTransactionID  341422 non-null  int64
 5   SalesItem           341422 non-null  int64
dtypes: datetime64[ns](1), float64(1), int64(4)
memory usage: 15.6 MB
```

# Check any number of columns with NaN or missing values
print(**data.isnull().any().sum()**, '/', len(**data.columns**))
# Check any number of data points with NaN
print(**data.isnull().any(axis=1).sum()**, '/', len(**data**))

```
0 / 8
0 / 341422
```

Let us get a first insight into our timeframe
data['SalesDate'].describe()

```
count                   341422
unique                    1008
top        2018-02-20 00:00:00
freq                       927
first      2016-05-02 00:00:00
last       2020-01-31 00:00:00
Name: SalesDate, dtype: object
```

This is also a key lesson we just learned: reading any messages
(like FutureWarning as above) Python is throwing at us. We will act
accordingly for the sake of getting rid of this message
data['SalesDate'].describe(datetime_is_numeric=True)

```
count                           341422
mean     2018-02-01 13:10:30.138641152
min                2016-05-02 00:00:00
25%                2017-02-14 00:00:00
50%                2018-01-02 00:00:00
75%                2019-01-08 00:00:00
max                2020-01-31 00:00:00
Name: SalesDate, dtype: object
```

Count is just the number of datasets (since we do not have any
NaN values). Mean is of no use for this date field. But with the
Min, Max, and Percentiles, we can already get a glimpse of the
date`s distribution. Because we are looking at the DateTime
field, it is more helpful to visually inspect this timeline on
SalesAmount later on.

data['SalesAmount'].describe()

```
count      341422.000000
mean            8.208209
std            35.476935
min             1.000000
25%             1.000000
50%             2.000000
75%             5.000000
max          2110.000000
Name: SalesAmount, dtype: float64
```

Df.describe(): the describe function works properly, if your data is already cleaned up. That means all fields are numeric, and there are no missing inputs.

We have to consider any NaN values and decide how to deal with them. Sometimes, it is a fair approach to replace them with a mean or average or even delete the whole datapoint. This decision always depends on your data!

SalesDate and SalesAmount can be better visually inspected than only looking at the describe function. For this reason, we import the two libraries, Seaborn and Matplotlib. Matplotlib is a library famous for mathematical plots (if you should have wondered where the name comes from). Seaborn puts more cherry on the cake, offering advanced visualizations based on Matplotlib. For convenience, we use short aliases like sns and plt (we can call them whatever we want, but it is good practice to use these well-known aliases).

```
#plotting to see distribution and find outliers visually
import seaborn as sns
import matplotlib.pyplot as plt
sns.distplot(data.SalesAmount.dropna())
plt.title('Distribution of Sales Quantity')
```

124

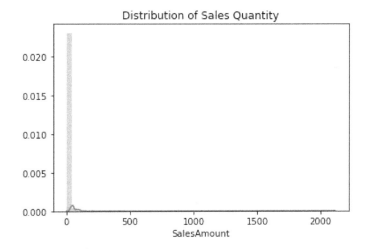
Distribution of Sales Quantity

As we can see, Seaborn and Matplotlib work together so that we can plot a histogram simply like that. Our distribution is highly right-skewed. Most of our sales Quantity is roughly between 0 and 200, and above are some extraordinary data points. Anomaly detection is about finding uncommon things, which we should always take care of during our EDA and data wrangling part.

```
#doing the same, but this time dynamically to improve data
understanding. Plotly makes a interactive histogram while seaborn
is just static:
import plotly.offline as pyoff
import plotly.graph_objs as go
plot_data = [
  go.Histogram(
    x=data['SalesAmount']
  )
]
plot_layout = go.Layout(
    title='SalesAmount'
  )
fig = go.Figure(data=plot_data, layout=plot_layout)
pyoff.iplot(fig)
```

using plotly we can now mouse over the bars to see the values. We can even zoom into our visualization for better scalability.

# using skewness and kurtosis as a statistical add to the above histogram to the shape of the distribution
print("Skewness: %f" % data['SalesAmount'].skew())
print("Kurtosis: %f" % data['SalesAmount'].kurt())

Skewness: 18.073516
Kurtosis: 440.674856

The skewness value is positive because the distribution tail is longer towards the right-hand side of the curve. It is not symmetrically distributed. Kurtosis measures whether the data is heavy-tailed or light-tailed relative to a normal distribution. Data sets with high kurtosis tend to have heavy tails or outliers.

#Just for the fun of it -and for learning purposes- we can achieve the same result if we add the function to a variable name (case sensitive!)
SkewValue = data.skew()
print("SkewValue of dataframe attributes: ", SkewValue)

```
SkewValue of dataframe attributes:  SalesValue          15.466199
SalesAmount           18.073516
Customer              -1.469180
SalesTransactionID     1.885978
SalesItem              1.452359
dtype: float64
```

#For a quick general overview for any possible correlation we can also use Seaborn`s pairplot function. This scatter plot matrix is useful for exploring the relationships between groups of continuous features. Please note, that there is no sense in plotting the keys for Customer, SalesTransactionID and SalesItems. We just do it to see how it would look like.
sns.pairplot(data, diag_kind="kde")
# diag_kind: Kind of plot for the diagonal subplots, kde: kernel

density estimate

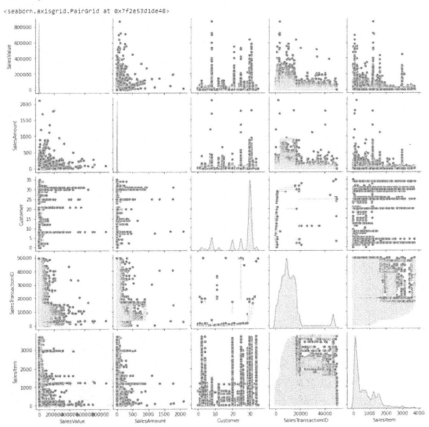

Better than a histogram, you can spot the overall distribution regarding Min, Max, Mean/Median, and Standard Deviation using a Box Plot or Violin Graph. Please note that this is quite resource-intensive:

fig=px.violin(data, x="Year", y="SalesAmount",box=True, points='all')

#simply pass "colab" as the value for the parameter renderer in fig.show(renderer="colab")

fig.show(renderer="colab")

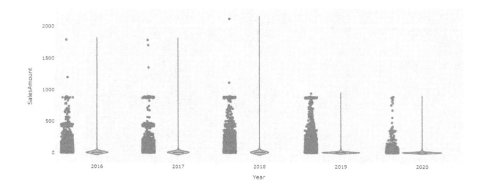

Until now, we have undertaken several steps to get a first glimpse of our data. There is also an excellent library that checks for data quality and distribution in a convenient way, called Ydata-profiling (formerly known as Pandas profiling). We can import it directly into our Jupyter Notebook in Colab like this:

```
#The autoreload instruction reloads modules automatically before code execution, which is helpful for the update below.
%load_ext autoreload
%autoreload 2
```

```
#Make sure that we have the latest version of pandas-profiling.
import sys
!{sys.executable} -m pip install -U pandas-profiling[notebook]
!jupyter nbextension enable --py widgetsnbextension
```

Requirement already up-to-date: pandas-profiling[notebook] in /usr/local/lib/python3.6/dist-packages (2.9.0)
Requirement already satisfied, skipping upgrade: tqdm>=4.43.0 in /usr/local/lib/python3.6/dist-packages (from pandas-profiling[notebook]) (4.40.0)
Requirement already satisfied, skipping upgrade: htmlmin>=0.1.12 in /usr/local/lib/python3.6/dist-packages (from pandas-profiling[notebook]) (0.1.12)
Requirement already satisfied, skipping upgrade: pandas!=1.0.0,!=1.0.1,!=1.0.1,!=1.1.0,0.>=0.25.3 in /usr/local/lib/python3.6/dist-packages (from pandas-profiling[notebook]) (1.0.5)

```
from pathlib import Path
import requests
import numpy as np
import pandas as pd
import pandas_profiling
from pandas_profiling.utils.cache import cache_file
```

/usr/local/lib/python3.6/dist-packages/statsmodels/tools/_testing.py:19: FutureWarning: pandas.util.testing is deprecated. Use the functions in the public API at pandas.testing instead.
  import pandas.util.testing as tm

```
#Inline report without saving object
report = data.profile_report(sort='None', html={'style':{'full_width':
True}}, progress_bar=False)
report
#Use this cell, if you want to save the report as a html file
profile_report = data.profile_report(html={'style': {'full_width':
True}})
profile_report.to_file("/PandasProf.html")
```

Hint:

if you use Jupyter Notebook on your machine, this will work:

import sys

!{sys.executable} -m pip install pandas-profiling

And run one line of code afterwards:

import pandas as pd

import pandas_profiling

pd.read_excel(DDDD.xlsx').profile_report()

df = pd.read_excel('DDDD.xlsx').profile_report()

df.to_file("DataProfiling.html")

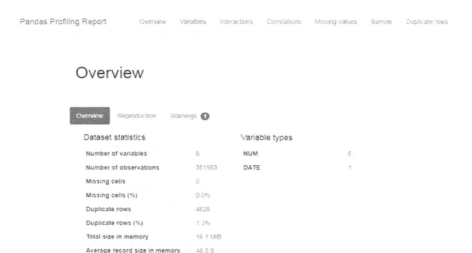

We can check warnings for NaN (not a number) or duplicate values, etc, in the tab "Warnings":

SalesAmount Real number ($\mathbb{R}_{\geq 0}$)	Distinct count	505	Mean	8.261276823021	
	Unique (%)	0.1%	Minimum	1	
	Missing	0	Maximum	2110	
	Missing (%)	0.0%	Zeros	0	
	Infinite	0	Zeros (%)	0.0%	
	Infinite (%)	0.0%	Memory size	2.7 MiB	

Toggle details

Inspecting our data visually helps us see the big picture more easily:

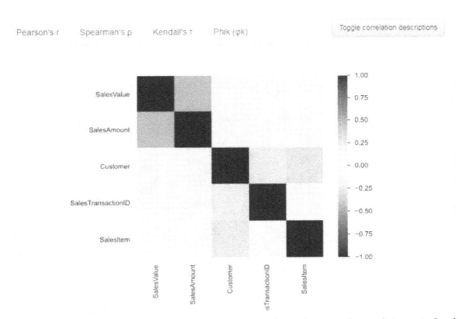

Not surprisingly, Sales Amount and Sales Value (Net Sales) are highly correlated (the more quantity of a specific product we sell, the higher the sales value/net sales). In general, the correlation coefficient is a metric that measures the extent to which numeric variables are associated with one another. It is a standardized metric that ranges from −1 (perfect negative correlation) to +1 (perfect positive correlation). A correlation

131

coefficient of 0 indicates no correlation.

The rest of this heatmap (correlation between SalesItem, Customer, and SalesTransactionID) is meaningless. Panda Profiling can not understand that customerID is simply a code for customers without any numerical meaning other than being used as a key to map with customer names later on. It is still our job to ensure that our analysis makes sense.

Our data set does not include any missing values:

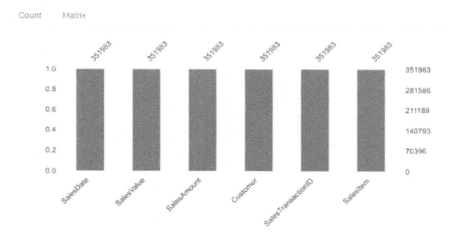

Most datasets are unique regarding their SalesTransactionID, but there are some exceptions (as usual). Check the overview "Most frequent" for more details:

Most frequent

	SalesDate	SalesValue	SalesAmount	Customer	SalesTransactionID	SalesItem	count
2116	2018-11-30	1839.07	1	8	2380	73	50
2115	2018-11-30	1839.07	1	8	2368	73	42
2	2016-03-29	284.66	1	8	3808	194	41
2123	2018-11-30	1866.11	1	8	2380	74	38
2122	2018-11-30	1866.11	1	8	2368	74	30
1073	2017-06-30	1793.96	1	8	3278	161	26
2484	2020-01-03	110.77	1	20	9844	1192	24
1385	2017-09-29	9392.28	5	8	3139	179	22
2423	2019-10-25	208.88	1	20	10347	104	21
1378	2017-09-29	493.15	5	8	3139	110	20

With just one line of code, we get a bunch of different descriptions of our data. That is already an impressive demonstration of why we will use packages a lot: we do not need to hardcode every function by ourselves, but we can instead call a library`s function and receive a pile of different results with just one shot. This impressively underlines the performance and usability benefits of using libraries.

Note that checking for unusual or extraordinary data points is essential because they might lead to wrong models and misleading assumptions. Data quality is critical; therefore, data wrangling must come before any model training.

Check for unusual values within the time series:

```
!pip install plotly_express
import plotly_express as px

DailySalesSum=data.resample('D', on='SalesDate').sum() #group on a daily 'D' basis; notice: SalesDate is not a column any longer, but an index
DailySalesSum.head()
```

SalesDate	SalesValue	SalesAmount	Customer	SalesTransactionID	SalesItem
2016-05-02	676484.17	3623	14241	8472690	361020
2016-05-03	411892.57	1910	7243	5582178	170648
2016-05-04	3112075.11	4758	11305	6641265	295923
2016-05-05	349020.52	1004	8294	4513983	266972
2016-05-06	1723892.93	2965	11290	8665817	354422

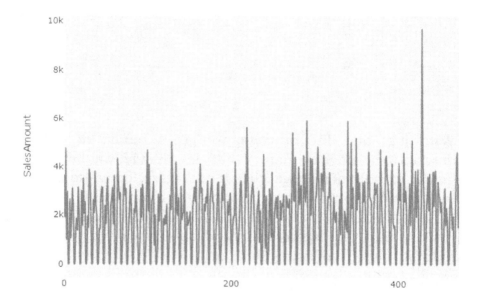

We can see two important things here. First, our time series is indexed (sequenced) sales quantities over time (x-axis). Second, we have many days with 0 sales quantity. In the next step, we will group monthly to get a better overall impression.

```
# we need to reset the index after resampling
DailySalesSum = DailySalesSum.reset_index()
DailySalesSum.head()
```

	SalesDate	SalesValue	SalesAmount	Customer	SalesTransactionID	SalesItem
0	2016-05-02	676484.17	3623	14241	8472690	361020
1	2016-05-03	411892.57	1910	7243	5582178	170648
2	2016-05-04	3112075.11	4758	11305	6641265	295923
3	2016-05-05	349020.52	1004	8294	4513983	266972
4	2016-05-06	1723892.93	2965	11290	8665817	354422

MonthlySalesSum=data.resample('M', on='SalesDate').sum() # M stands for Month End, in contrast to MS-Month Start
MonthlySalesSum = MonthlySalesSum.reset_index()
MonthlySalesSum.head()

	SalesDate	SalesValue	SalesAmount	Customer	SalesTransactionID	SalesItem
0	2016-05-31	20166177.78	51265	219003	147309836	5878767
1	2016-06-30	20092795.13	56692	236608	164558983	6267283
2	2016-07-31	19127473.54	53954	234838	181719685	6182682
3	2016-08-31	19677492.02	55496	246380	181872656	6316045
4	2016-09-30	19663361.67	53552	230070	169774628	6271814

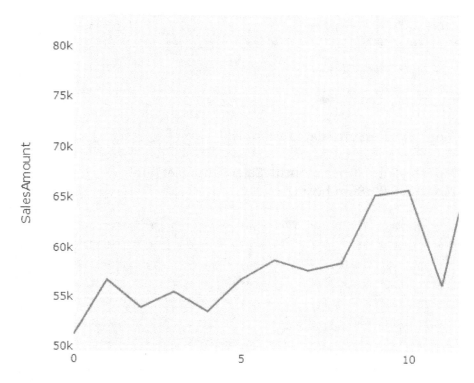

As promised, monthly sales look much cleaner than daily sales. Let's stick to this grouping idea a little longer, this time calculating mean instead of sum for daily, weekly, monthly, quarterly, and yearly levels.

# Instead of the above cells, we can also do it all in one cell via creating one DF for grouping on time series
TimeSeriesGroup = data.set_index('SalesDate')
TimeSeriesGroup=TimeSeriesGroup.drop(columns=['SalesValue','Customer','SalesTransactionID','SalesItem'])
#TimeSeriesGroup = TimeSeriesGroup.resample('d').mean()

This time we will calculate the mean (insted of sums) and then plot five diagrams.
I would always stick to summing our sales amount instead of averaging. Using average will result in loss of information. But for

learning purpose we will give mean a try here. And we can also see that average smoothens our data, which can be a very supportive thing.

```
fig, (ax1,ax2,ax3,ax4,ax5) = plt.subplots(5,figsize=(30,15))
```

```
# note that all days in between our time series get plotted, even if no
sales exist. That's the reason for the many 0 values.
ax1.plot(TimeSeriesGroup['SalesAmount'].resample('D').mean())
ax1.set_title('Daily');

ax2.plot(TimeSeriesGroup['SalesAmount'].resample('W').mean())
ax2.set_title('Weekly');

ax3.plot(TimeSeriesGroup['SalesAmount'].resample('M').mean())
ax3.set_title('Monthly');

ax4.plot(TimeSeriesGroup['SalesAmount'].resample('Q').mean())
ax4.set_title('Quarterly');

ax5.plot(TimeSeriesGroup['SalesAmount'].resample('A').mean())
ax5.set_title('Yearly');
# Daily data has at least two extreme outliers. Remember that
average values are highly influenced by outliers.
# Scale gets much clearer looking the weekly averages.
# Looking from monthly over quarterly to yearly average we can
clearly see the overall rising trend.
```

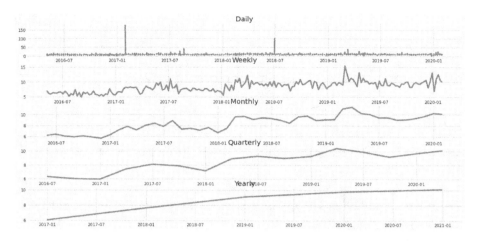

Remember when we briefly discussed SPC in chapter 1.1.1? By looking at the weekly mean and standard deviation, we can see how the location and variance change over time.

fig, (ax1,ax2,ax3,ax4) = plt.subplots(4,figsize=(30,15))

ax1.plot(TimeSeriesGroup['SalesAmount'].resample('W').sum())
ax1.set_title('Weekly Sum');

ax2.plot(TimeSeriesGroup['SalesAmount'].resample('W').mean())
ax2.set_title('Weekly Average');

ax3.plot(TimeSeriesGroup['SalesAmount'].resample('W').std())
ax3.set_title('Weekly Standard Deviation');

ax4.plot(TimeSeriesGroup['SalesAmount'].resample('W').median())
ax4.set_title('Weekly Median');

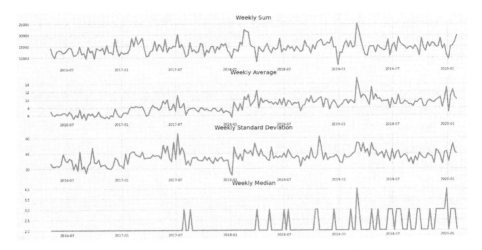

Statistical Process Control (SPC) can be very helpful in production processes (automated and stable processes) where you work with control limits. Regarding our sales data, SPC is only of limited use because our sales do not obey any specifications, and we cannot control the standard deviations and shifts of our sales data. But we can still use this technique for detailed discussions with our sales colleagues without arguing about any control limits (you should have sold more than x quantities on average last week due to weeks before that).

After this little digression into SPC, we will return to our time series grouping. Besides just grouping, we can also calculate the development between different timestamps. For instance, we can calculate the increase/decrease between weekday, month, and year sales:

AnomalyTimeSeriesDoW=AnomalyTimeSeries.groupby(Anomaly TimeSeries.index.dayofweek).sum().reset_index().rename(column s={"SalesDate": "Day", "SalesAmount": "SalesAmountSum"}) AnomalyTimeSeriesDoW.set_index("Day", drop=True, inplace=True)

AnomalyTimeSeriesMonth=AnomalyTimeSeries.groupby(Anomal yTimeSeries.index.month).sum().reset_index().rename(columns={

```
"SalesDate": "Month", "SalesAmount": "SalesAmountSum"})
AnomalyTimeSeriesMonth.set_index("Month",          drop=True,
inplace=True)


AnomalyTimeSeriesYear=AnomalyTimeSeries.groupby(AnomalyT
imeSeries.index.year).sum().reset_index().rename(columns={"Sales
Date": "Year", "SalesAmount": "SalesAmountSum"})
AnomalyTimeSeriesYear.set_index("Year",          drop=True,
inplace=True)


AnomalyTimeSeriesDoW['PercentageIncrease']=(AnomalyTimeSer
iesDoW.pct_change().fillna(0))*100
AnomalyTimeSeriesMonth['PercentageIncrease']=AnomalyTimeSe
riesMonth.pct_change().fillna(0)*100
AnomalyTimeSeriesYear['PercentageIncrease']=AnomalyTimeSerie
sYear.pct_change().fillna(0)*100


fig, (ax1, ax2,ax3) = plt.subplots(3,figsize=(30,15))
ax1.plot(AnomalyTimeSeriesDoW.PercentageIncrease,marker='o',
linestyle='--')
ax1.set_title('Weekly Percentage Increase (starting with monday at
index 0)');
ax2.plot(AnomalyTimeSeriesMonth.PercentageIncrease,marker='o'
, linestyle='--')
ax2.set_title('Monthly Percentage Increase ');
ax3.plot(AnomalyTimeSeriesYear.PercentageIncrease,marker='o',
linestyle='--')
ax3.set_title('Yearly Percentage Increase');
```

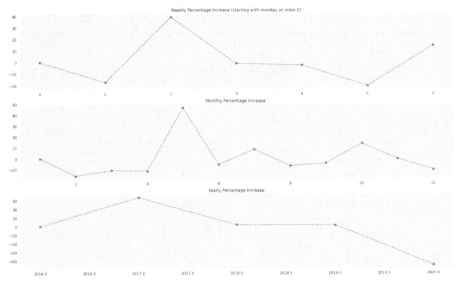

Let us look at the day of the week graph to explain how to interpret the first graph: Monday is index 0 and has an overall SalesAmount of 391,837. Tuesday is at index one and has 324,108 quantities sold. That means, from Monday to Tuesday, we have a decrease of -17.28%:

```
AnomalyTimeSeriesDoW
# from Monday to Tuesday: (391837-324108)/391837 =17% (decrease)
```

	SalesAmountSum	PercentageIncrease
Day		
0	391837	0.000000
1	324108	-17.284994
2	451723	39.374221
3	447677	-0.895682
4	437262	-2.326454
5	349139	-20.153363
6	400717	14.772913

Moving average (also called rolling average/mean) calculates the mathematical average of a rolling window of a defined width. It is one the most frequently and simplest statistical models used for forecasting (see chapter 2.3). The idea is that future values are similar to the recent values we observed. Below, we calculate the moving average, e.g., the last two months, so our window is 2. That means we need at least two months to calculate something. While this may be logical to you, it is an essential aspect of any model called **Initialization.** Only if we have enough observations (data from the past) can we initialize any model. If we use the moving AverageAverage to predict future values, we will only receive a flat prediction (every future value will remain the same). We will use more advanced techniques than the moving AverageAverage in chapter 2.3 to predict.

Exponential smoothing (also called exponentially weighted) uses the exponential (as the weight given to each observation is exponentially reduced) window function and is frequently used in analyzing time series. Meanwhile, past observations are weighted equally in the simple moving average, and exponential functions assign exponentially decreasing weights over time. In other words, this model assumes that the current past values substantially influence future values more than elderly data. Exponential smoothing adds level (not to be confused by seasonality; see next page triple exponential smoothing) to the model (compared to a more straightforward moving average). The **level** is the average value around which our sales quantity varies over time, so the level is just a smoothed version of past sales quantities. Exponential smoothing models always learn from the most recent sales quantity, remembering a bit of the last forecast because the last forecast includes a part of the previous actual sales quantity and a part of the earlier forecast. The smoothing parameter (or **learning rate**) alpha will determine the importance of the most recent actual sales quantity. High alpha means that the model will allocate more significance to the most current sales quantities (the model being very responsive but also prone to noise). The weight put on each sales quantity from the past decreases exponentially over time, meaning most current sales quantities have the highest weight. This often is a benefit compared to moving average models.

We must also be aware of **data leakage** here. If we choose an initialization method that includes information about multiple periods ahead, we will cheat on ourselves because we will give our model too much information about the future (overfitting).

Since exponential smoothing does not project trends, we will use **double exponential smoothing** to solve this disadvantage.

Triple exponential smoothing adds even **seasonal** patterns to our model. However, none of these exponential statistical models can add external features (like discounts, sales events, etc.), which only ML models can do. As a last note, we need to choose the window width carefully. A too-narrow window will react quickly to changing sales amounts but is also more likely to overfitting due to noise in our data. On the other hand, a window size that is too large can over-smooth our sales series, perishing the seasonal effect (if any). We should always try to find a good balance between (trade-off between reactivity and smoothness).

just for learning purpose we add two variables to filter our time

series for start and end date:
```
start, end = '2016-04-01', '2020-02-01'

fig, ax = plt.subplots(figsize=(30,15))

ax.plot(AnomalyTimeSeries.loc[start:end],
marker='o', markersize=8, linestyle='-', label='Actual',color='k')

ax.plot(AnomalyTimeSeries.rolling(window=2,center=True).mean
().loc[start:end],
marker='o',              markersize=8,              linestyle='--',
label='RollingMean2',color='g')

ax.plot(AnomalyTimeSeries.rolling(window=10,center=True).mea
n().loc[start:end],
marker='o',              markersize=8,              linestyle='--',
label='RollingMean10',color='r')

ax.plot(AnomalyTimeSeries.rolling(window=5,
win_type='gaussian',center=True).mean(std=10).loc[start:end],
marker='o', linestyle='--', label='Gaussian',color='c')

ax.plot(AnomalyTimeSeries.rolling(window=5,center=True).mean
().loc[start:end],
marker='o',  linestyle='--', label='RollingMean',color='m')

ax.plot(AnomalyTimeSeries.ewm(span=5).mean().loc[start:end],
marker='o',                                    linestyle='--',
label='ExponentialWeighted',color='magenta')

ax.set_ylabel('SalesAmount')
ax.legend();
```

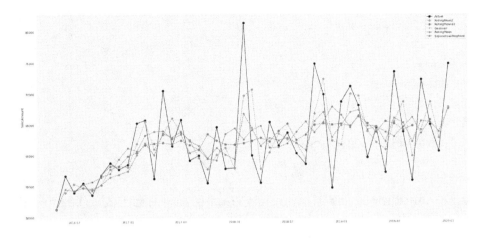

We looked at the daily, weekly, etc. sums per time, but now we want to use a more target-oriented technique to spot any unusual quantities (also called anomaly or outlier detection).

#Anomaly Detection: spotting unusual data points
AnomalyTimeSeries = data.set_index('SalesDate')
AnomalyTimeSeries=AnomalyTimeSeries.drop(columns=['SalesVa lue','Customer','SalesTransactionID','SalesItem'])
AnomalyTimeSeries = AnomalyTimeSeries.resample('MS').sum() # grouping SalesAmount on a monthly basis, for each Month Start 'MS'
# in case you want to resample (group) not on a yearly or weekly level instead
#AnomalyTimeSeries = AnomalyTimeSeries.resample('W').sum() # weekly level
#AnomalyTimeSeries = AnomalyTimeSeries.resample('AS').sum() #yearly level
AnomalyTimeSeries.head()

	SalesAmount
SalesDate	
2016-05-01	51265
2016-06-01	56692
2016-07-01	53954
2016-08-01	55496
2016-09-01	53552

AnomalyTimeSeries = AnomalyTimeSeries.reset_index().dropna()
#resetting index, so we get back two columns again
AnomalyTimeSeries.columns = ['ds', 'y'] #we will use a Package called Prophet later on on this, which needs the input to be called ds for time and y for our SalesAmount
AnomalyTimeSeries.head()

	ds	y
0	2016-05-01	51265
1	2016-06-01	56692
2	2016-07-01	53954
3	2016-08-01	55496
4	2016-09-01	53552

AnomalyTimeSeries.columns = ['ds', 'y']
fig = plt.figure(facecolor='w', figsize=(20, 6))
plt.plot(AnomalyTimeSeries.ds, AnomalyTimeSeries.y)

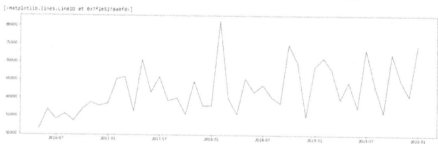

#Using Prophet to spot unusual data points: black dots are actual data points, blue line is predicted by Facebook`s Prophet, and blue shade represents 95% confidence interval: any black dotted actuals outside the blue shade can be estimated as extraordinary values within this specific time series

```
from fbprophet import Prophet
from fbprophet.plot import plot_plotly
import plotly.offline as py
py.init_notebook_mode()
m = Prophet(seasonality_mode='additive',interval_width=0.95).fit(AnomalyTimeSeries) #additive vs multiplicative seasonality, 95% Konfidenzintervall
future = m.make_future_dataframe(periods=0, freq='MS')# replace 0 by eg 12, to make a prediction for the next 12 months; vs just periods=365 --> which works well for weekly and daily
fcst = m.predict(future)
fig = plot_plotly(m,fcst)
#py.iplot(fig) #use this locally
#fig.show #or use this locally
fig.show(renderer="colab") #use this if you run it on Colab
```

INFO:fbprophet:Disabling weekly seasonality. Run prophet with weekly_seasonality=True to override this.
INFO:fbprophet:Disabling daily seasonality. Run prophet with daily_seasonality=True to override this.

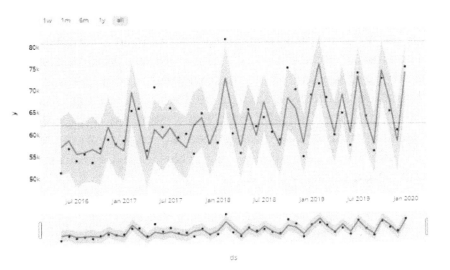

Of course, there is no absolute right or wrong regarding whether a data point is unusual. It just strongly depends, and only the human expert can tell. Only she has the domain expertise to know if

this data point is wrongly entered or just too extraordinary, so we should delete it before feeding it to the model.

We can also use Prophet's component function to check for trend and seasonality.

```
from fbprophet.plot import plot_plotly, plot_components_plotly
fig2=plot_components_plotly(m, fcst)
fig2.show(renderer="colab")
#in case you want to display the chart static
#fig2 = m.plot_components(fcst)
```

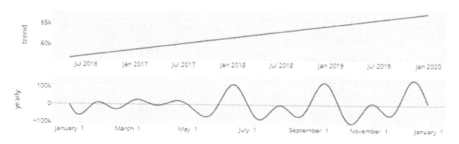

What exactly does that mean? We will analyze the time series, building a statistical model to answer that question. The above cells are most helpful in gathering a pragmatic understanding of the time series data points. However, we would only notice something if we looked at the statistical model in more detail. This statistical model is also an outlook for the sales prediction in the chapter "Sales Prediction" later on since SARIMA (Seasonal Autoregressive Integrated Moving Average) will build an excellent bridge between descriptive statistics and trying to predict future sales with ML.

```
# from Prophet we will move to the descriptive statistics of our time
series using Statsmodels
df3=data.drop(columns=[ 'SalesValue','Customer','SalesTransaction
ID','SalesItem', 'Year','Month'])
df3['SalesDate'] = pd.to_datetime(df3['SalesDate'])
```

```
df3 = df3.set_index('SalesDate')
daily_df = df3.resample('MS').sum()#D vs resample(ms); M monthly
vs D daily ws weekly w, M End of month, MS start of month
d_df = daily_df.reset_index().dropna()
d_df.columns = ['ds', 'y']
fig = plt.figure(facecolor='w', figsize=(20, 6))
plt.plot(d_df.ds, d_df.y)
```

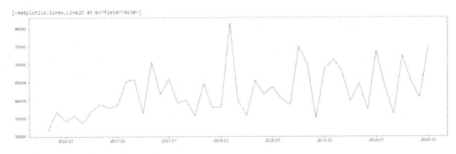

Looking at the "time series sales quantity" line chart in more detail, we need to understand the meaning of level, trend, seasonality, and residual.

Level: the average value in the series

Trend: any increasing or decreasing level moving

Seasonality: represents the repetition of a specific pattern in a seasonal manner (after some time periods, think of Christmas sales)

Residual: the difference between the actual and predicted (fitted) sales quantities. A suitable forecasting method will yield residuals with the following properties:

1. The residuals are uncorrelated. If there are correlations between residuals, then information is left in the residuals that should be used in computing forecasts. For instance, if, for any reason, the sales quantity in March always has a substantial impact on sales quantities in June (high correlation, not causation), then the model should be able to reveal this (and so finally leave uncorrelated residuals behind).

2. The residuals have zero mean, which means that the residuals are random. If the residuals have a mean other

than zero, then the forecasts are biased (bias is not to be confused with noise, which is just the inevitable random variation in the series).

We will see what that means for our data concretely shortly.

```
import statsmodels.api as sm
from pandas.testing import assert_frame_equal
from pylab import rcParams
rcParams['figure.figsize'] = 15, 6
decomposition       =       sm.tsa.seasonal_decompose(daily_df,
model='additive')#multiplicative cannot be used instead of additive
anyway!
#An additive (model is made up of observed, trend, seasonal and
residual (noise) components) model is linear where changes over
time are consistently made by the same amount. A linear trend is a
straight line. A linear seasonality has the same frequency (width of
cycles) and amplitude (height of cycles).
fig = decomposition.plot()
plt.show()
#trend is associated with the slope (increasing/decreasing) of the
time series
#seasonality  is the deviations from the mean caused by repeating
short-term cycles and
#noise is the random variation in the series
```

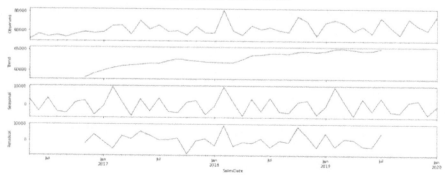

Only systematic components (consistency) of the time series can be modeled. We model the time series with the four components above. We see an overall positive trend and a high seasonal peak during February. The residuals are also interesting, showing periods of higher variability from September to November 2017, January to March 2018, and September to November 2018.

Most statistical models need the time series to be **stationary,** to be effective. A time series is considered stationary if the mean and variance are consistent over time. In other words, our SalesAmount is not dependent on time and shows no trend or seasonal effects. Also, covariance must be independent of time. We have seen an upward trend, so it is not a stationary time series. Also, the variance is changing, violating against being stationary data (variance is changing is also called volatility). Even if this is not stationary, we can still make different transformations to make our data stationary.

```
# Now we will use a statistic model to make inferences on the
time series
from statsmodels.tsa.stattools import adfuller, kpss


# The null hypothesis in the Augmented Dickey-Fuller test
(ADF) test tells us non-stationary. If p-value is less than the
significance level
# (0.05) we will reject the null hypothesis (meaning the series
has no unit root and is stationary). Unit root test uses an
autoregressive model and optimizes across multiple different
lag values, finally to determine how strong our time series is
influenced by a trend.
result         =         adfuller(AnomalyTimeSeries['SalesAmount'],
autolag='AIC')
print(f'ADF Statistic: {result[0]}')
print(f'p-value: {result[1]}')
```

```
if result[1] > 0.05:

  print('Series is not Stationary')

else:

  print('Series is Stationary')
```

```python
# Null hypothesis of KPSS Test tells us that our time series is
stationary.
stats,        p,        lags,        critical_values        =
kpss(AnomalyTimeSeries['SalesAmount'], 'ct')
print(f'KPSS Test Statistics: {stats}')
print(f'p-value: {p}')
```

```
if p<0.05:

    print('Series is not Stationary')

else:

    print('Series is Stationary')
```

ADF Statistic: -4.583215711105715

p-value: 0.0001386903323300616

Series is Stationary

KPSS Test Statistics: 0.1272560285196136

p-value: 0.08471105829701185

Series is Stationary

Even if the data were not stationary, there are several ways to solve this. See enforce_stationary in the next cell.

We do not need to log our data, because it does seem to be stationary. In case it would not, we can log transform our data to make the distribution of our SalesAmount more linear

from numpy import log

We use log if data has unequal variances.

LogAnomalyTimeSeries = log(AnomalyTimeSeries['SalesAmount'])

result = adfuller(LogAnomalyTimeSeries)

print('ADF Statistic: %f' % result[0])

print('p-value: %f' % result[1])

As already mentioned, the sequence order of our time series is an important aspect. This sequence order can contain extra information: do current values have a stronger impact on the next month's sales amount, or does last year's datapoint influence today's datapoint more strongly than yesterday's one, etc (seasonal influence)? Autocorrelation can help us to determine this because it can help us discover patterns in our time series and successfully select the best modeling algorithm. Specifically, autocorrelation and partial autocorrelation plots are heavily used to summarize the strength and relationship within observations in a time series with observations at prior time steps. When there is a strong seasonal pattern, we can see in the ACF (Autocorrelation Function) plot that repeated spikes are usually determined at the multiples of the seasonal window (think of a spike at the 12th month in most monthly sales time series). We can calculate the correlation between time series observations and observations from previous time steps, which are called **lags.** For instance, if we group the sales on a monthly level and expect next month's sales to be exactly like this month, then our prediction is our current sales with a one-period (month in our case) lag.

This "next month will just be like the current month" is also called a **naive forecast**. If our model estimates data points close to the predicted values in time have a substantial impact, our model will react quickly to changing circumstances. But on the other hand, our model is also more likely to be sensitive to noise and outliers (overfitting, see chapter 1.1.2). **Noise** in statistics is just the unexplained variation in which every process inheres.

```
from statsmodels.tsa.stattools import acf, pacf

from statsmodels.graphics.tsaplots import plot_acf, plot_pacf

import matplotlib.pyplot as plt


#Because the correlation of the time series observations is
calculated with values of the same series at previous times, this
is called a serial correlation, or an autocorrelation.

#The coefficient of correlation between two values in a time
series is called the autocorrelation function (ACF),

#and an ACF plot is a visual representation of correlations
between different lags.

# Calculate AutoCorrelation Function (ACF) and PACF upto 25
lags

acf_25 = acf(AnomalyTimeSeries['y'], nlags=25)

pacf_25 = pacf(AnomalyTimeSeries['y'], nlags=25)


# Draw Plot

fig, axes = plt.subplots(1,2,figsize=(16,3), dpi= 100)

plot_acf(acf_25, lags=25, ax=axes[0])

plot_pacf(pacf_25, lags=25, ax=axes[1])
```

the blue shaded horizontal cone represents the confidence level (here 95%). In other words, if the point is outside the cone (on white) you may say that with 95% probability is has a certain impact on values. If the bar is inside the cone (on blue) you may ignore this particular lag as most likely it is not relevant. The first bar is 1. This indexed 0 has always 1, since the first value always explains itself by 100%. The second point is around -0.1 which means that the directly next value is described in -10% by the previous value. The eleventh bar has a height of appr -0.4. This means that current data will impact data in 11 months by -40%. A negative autocorrelation implies that if a past value is above average the newer value is more likely to be below average (vice versa). This means, if this month we observe > average(SalesAmount), we might say that with 40% probability in 10 months we will gather less SalesAmount than on average.

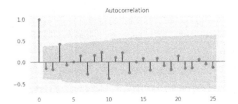
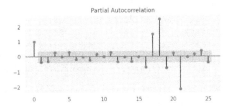

ACF and PACF can determine the number of autoregressors and moving average terms needed to make a model. These two terms come from the theory that the time series's formula comprises different parts of an autoregression (next value somewhat based on the previous), the moving average (the average of the noise in a model in a prior and current time), and the noise. A time series can have any number of these, so we look at the ACF and PACF plots to reiterate. Using autocorrelation, we can find patterns in our sales data. This statistical modeling technique is also building a bridge to our deep learning forecasting later on because we can make more efficient and less computationally expensive models (you don't need this "trick" if your machine is sufficient enough) by ignoring values (creating smaller learning batches) that statistically do not have an impact on data.

Now, let us build our statistical model and see if we can fit the data's patterns.

```
#import statsmodels.api as sm
mod = sm.tsa.statespace.SARIMAX(daily_df,
            order=(1, 1, 1),
            seasonal_order=(1, 1, 0, 12),
            enforce_stationarity=False,
            enforce_invertibility=False)
results = mod.fit()
print(results.summary().tables[1])
```

	coef	std err	z	P>|z|	[0.025	0.975]
ar.L1	-0.2212	0.570	-0.388	0.698	-1.338	0.896
ma.L1	-0.7108	0.236	-3.010	0.003	-1.174	-0.248
ar.S.L12	-0.2525	0.322	-0.785	0.432	-0.883	0.378
sigma2	5.999e+07	3.79e-10	1.58e+17	0.000	6e+07	6e+07

The coefficients (coef) column shows each feature's weight (i.e., importance) and how each one impacts the time series. The P>|z| column informs us of the significance of each feature weight. Only ma.L1 and sigma2 weights have a p-value lower or close to 0.05, so it is reasonable to retain only these in our model.

Enter results.summary() to get the full summary:

Statespace Model Results

Dep. Variable:	SalesAmount			No. Observations:	45
Model:	SARIMAX(1, 1, 1)x(1, 1, 0, 12)			Log Likelihood	-195.074
Date:	Fri, 04 Dec 2020			AIC	398.149
Time:	21:57:53			BIC	401.927
Sample:	05-01-2016			HQIC	398.788
	- 01-01-2020				
Covariance Type:	opg				

	coef	std err	z	P>|z|	[0.025	0.975]
ar.L1	-0.2212	0.570	-0.388	0.698	-1.338	0.896
ma.L1	-0.7108	0.236	-3.010	0.003	-1.174	-0.248
ar.S.L12	-0.2525	0.322	-0.785	0.432	-0.883	0.378
sigma2	5.999e+07	3.79e-10	1.58e+17	0.000	6e+07	6e+07

Ljung-Box (Q):	nan	Jarque-Bera (JB):	0.84
Prob(Q):	nan	Prob(JB):	0.66
Heteroskedasticity (H):	0.35	Skew:	0.47
Prob(H) (two-sided):	0.22	Kurtosis:	2.60

```
results.plot_diagnostics(figsize=(15, 12))
plt.show()
```

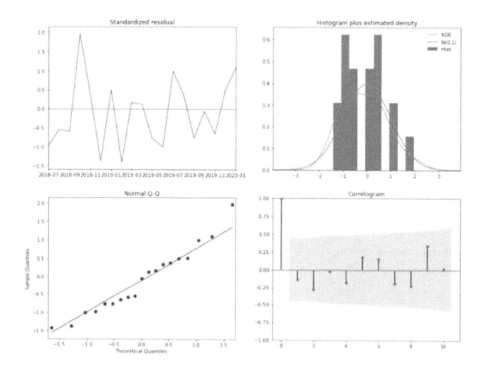

There seems to be a pattern in the "standardized residuals" left, indicating our model is imperfect. Because the residuals are not randomly scattered around zero for the entire range of fitted sales quantities (our residuals do not have a zero mean), the residual errors do not seem to fluctuate around a mean of zero and, therefore, do not have a uniform variance. Residual, indeed, is the difference between the true and predicted value. The residuals of our model should be uncorrelated and normally distributed with a zero mean. If the seasonal ARIMA model does not satisfy these properties, it is a good indication that it can be further improved. If there are correlations between residuals, information is left in the residuals that should be used in computing forecasts. If the residuals have a mean other than zero, then the forecasts are biased (meaning that our model does not entirely depict the process). In the top right plot, we see that the red KDE line follows closely with the N(0,1) line (where

N(0,1)) is the standard notation for a normal distribution with a mean of 0 and a standard deviation of 1). This is a good indication that the residuals are normally distributed. The qq-plot on the bottom left shows that the ordered distribution of residuals (blue dots) follows the linear trend of the samples taken from a standard normal distribution with N(0, 1). Again, this is a strong indication that the residuals are normally distributed. The residuals over time (top left plot) don't display any apparent seasonality and appear as white noise. This is confirmed by the autocorrelation (i.e., Correlogram) plot on the bottom right, which shows that the time series residuals have a low correlation with lagged versions of itself. Those observations lead us to conclude that our model produces a satisfactory fit that could help us understand our time series data and forecast future values. The density plot in the top right suggests a normal distribution with mean of zero. Most of the dots in the bottom left do not align with the red line. This implies that the distribution is skewed, as we were just made aware using the skew function. The Correlogram in the bottom right, aka ACF plot, shows the residual errors are not autocorrelated. Any autocorrelation would imply that there is some pattern in the residual errors, which are not explained in the model. So, it would help if you looked for more X's (predictors) in the model. In the Correlogram, we can see that neighboring residuals are not correlated, which is a good sign (one residual can not predict the next residual, which would be autocorrelation). The "Q-Q" and "Histogram" charts are fair enough, even though they are not perfectly normally distributed.

Even though there is room for improvement from a statistical point of view, we will now use this SARIMA model to plot the prediction against our actual values.

```
pred = results.get_prediction(start=pd.to_datetime('2019-05-01'),
dynamic=False)
pred_ci = pred.conf_int()
ax = daily_df['2016':].plot(label='observed')
```

```
pred.predicted_mean.plot(ax=ax,    label='Prediction',    alpha=.7,
figsize=(14, 7))
ax.fill_between(pred_ci.index,
        pred_ci.iloc[:, 0],
        pred_ci.iloc[:, 1], color='k', alpha=.2)
ax.set_xlabel('Month')
ax.set_ylabel('observed')
plt.legend()
plt.show()
```

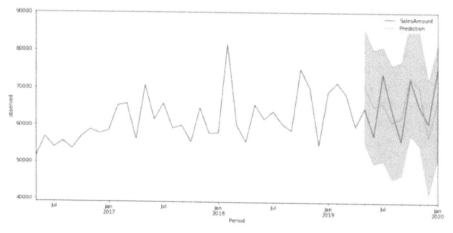

In the "Sales Prediction" chapter, we will use this statistical SARIMA model to predict sales quantity for future periods.

In this chapter, we explored our data to understand the shape and distribution and conducted data cleansing where necessary. We must remember that data quality is essential and must be checked and revised before training any models: our model can never overachieve poor data quality, no matter how hard we work on our model (garbage in, garbage out)! We also used descriptive statistics, specifically on our time series data, and set up a statistical model to best fit our past data. Only if we understand the past will we be able to predict future sales quantities.

2.2 RFM CLUSTERING

So far, we have used descriptive statistics to analyze our data. Now, we will calculate new date and sales-dependent key performance indicators (RFM KPI) and cluster them meaningfully. RFM is a clustering method that evaluates our customers based solely on their purchase history. The three RFM factors are:

Recency: amount of days since the last customer's purchase (sales)

Very recent customer clusters will need a different salesforce handling than very "outdated" clusters.

Frequency: how often customer is buying in a defined time frame

Combining frequency with sales quantity to show "ideally" sales frequencies (win win for both customer and our company?)

Monetary Value: the sum of net sales (for a defined time frame). Could also be exchanged by margin or average sales.

For example, salesforce actions will differ for high net sales clusters compared to lower ones. Out of these three measures, we can calculate an overall KPI:

R+F+M = **Overall RFM score**

Now, we can segment our customers into different groups, such as" champion customers," "inactive customers," "penny pincher customers," etc. In many businesses, the Pareto principle is also valid here: 80% of the sales come from 20% of the customers, so it makes sense to focus most of our attention on these 20% champion customers.

As a starting point, RFM is equal to all three. Depending on our sales colleagues' feedback, we can change the weight at any time (e.g., maybe Frequency is more vital to our sales domain than Recency so that we could add an extra 10% on frequency R +F*1,1+NetSales)

NextPurchaseDay: will the customer purchase/ place an order next week/month, etc.?

If, due to the customer's past behavior, we estimate him to buy next week anyway, there is no need for the sales team to spend additional effort on this customer. If this customer's next week purchase doesn't come in, salesforce should get active ("Dear Customer, usually you would have bought this week, but you haven't. Can we help you with anything..?).

Let us use Unsupervised ML for clustering. Clustering in plain English means that we try to put similar things together.

First we will check how many unique customers we have:

```
import pandas as pd
data = pd.read_excel('/content/gdrive/My Drive/DDDDFolder/DDDD.xlsx')
data['Customer'].nunique()
```

We will add these 35 unique customers to a column "customer" in a new dataframe "CustomerUnique":

```
CustUnique = pd.DataFrame(data['Customer'].unique())
CustUnique.columns = ['Customer']
```


Calculating **Recency**:

Sales data exists from May 2016 – January 2020, with 35 unique customers.

For Recency, we are checking the most current last purchase date (max date) for each customer, using a group by function:

```
MaxPurchaseDate                                          =
data.groupby('Customer').SalesDate.max().reset_index()
MaxPurchaseDate.columns = ['Customer','MaxPurchaseDate']
MaxPurchaseDate.head()
```

	Customer	MaxPurchaseDate
0	0	2019-12-23
1	1	2020-01-21
2	2	2020-01-29
3	3	2020-01-10
4	4	2020-01-29

```
#take the overall max date and calculate the difference in days for
each customer`s max date from that overall max date
MaxPurchaseDate['Recency']                               =
(MaxPurchaseDate['MaxPurchaseDate'].max()                -
MaxPurchaseDate['MaxPurchaseDate']).dt.days
CustUnique              =              pd.merge(CustUnique,
MaxPurchaseDate[['Customer','Recency']], on='Customer')
CustUnique.head()
```

	Customer	Recency
0	0	39
1	1	10
2	3	21
3	4	2
4	5	28

We can finally calculate the recency as a date difference between MaxPurchaseDate and the most current overall date. So, e.g., customer .. has a recency of .. days, since the last purchase date is .. and that is .. days off to .. (as most current overall purchase date):

CustUnique.Recency.describe()

```
count        35.000000
mean        132.000000
std         287.880592
min           0.000000
25%           1.500000
50%          16.000000
75%          52.000000
max        1032.000000
```

Let us have a look at recency's distribution:

```
import plotly.offline as pyoff
import plotly.graph_objs as go
plot_data = [
  go.Histogram(
    x=CustUnique['Recency']
  )
]
plot_layout = go.Layout(
    title='Recency'
  )
```

```
fig = go.Figure(data=plot_data, layout=plot_layout)
pyoff.iplot(fig)
```

Just by looking at the above chart, we can see that it is strongly right-skewed.

We will use unsupervised ML to set cluster criteria (without any domain knowledge: we will amend calculations of all KPI and statistics after we receive feedback from our salesforce colleagues). Since a cluster is a group of similar records, the mean (in K-Means) is the vector of variable means for the data points in a cluster. K stands for the number of clusters. K-means divides the data into k clusters by minimizing the sum of the squared distances of each record to the mean of its assigned cluster. This ensures we will find ideally separated clusters (but not necessarily having the same size in one cluster). Why do we use unsupervised ML and not just "simple" statistics like binning (binning involves converting continuous values into categories as a series of ranges)? Well, just because we can (and because we want to become familiar with unsupervised ML)!

```
import matplotlib.pyplot as plt
from sklearn.cluster import KMeans
inertia={}
tx_recency = CustUnique[['Recency']]
for k in range(1, 10):
    kmeans = KMeans(n_clusters=k, max_iter=1000).fit(tx_recency)
    tx_recency["clusters"] = kmeans.labels_
    inertia[k] = kmeans.inertia_
plt.figure(figsize=(10, 6))
```

```
plt.plot(list(inertia.keys()), list(inertia.values()), marker='o')
plt.xlabel("Number of cluster", fontsize=16)
plt.ylabel("Inertia", fontsize=16)
plt.xticks(list(inertia.keys()))
plt.show();
```

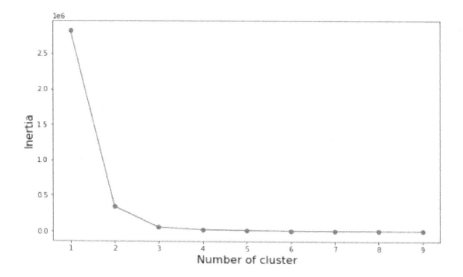

The **elbow** (the point where the cumulative variance explained flattens out after rising steeply) method identifies when the set of clusters explains most of the variance. As we can see, we will use 3 clusters since there is no extra benefit in using >=4 clusters (only relatively incremental contribution in the explained variance):

```
kmeans = KMeans(n_clusters=3)
kmeans.fit(CustUnique[['Recency']])
CustUnique['RecencyCluster']                                    =
kmeans.predict(CustUnique[['Recency']])

CustUnique.groupby('RecencyCluster')['Recency'].describe()
```

	count	mean	std	min	25%	50%	75%	max
RecencyCluster								
0	30.0	23.366667	38.534788	0.0	1.0	10.0	25.0	168.0
1	3.0	979.000000	72.794231	896.0	952.5	1009.0	1020.5	1032.0
2	2.0	491.000000	8.485281	485.0	488.0	491.0	494.0	497.0

This means cluster 0, for instance, includes 30 customers whose last purchase was 23 days ago (average). Cluster 1 is the most outdated cluster, with an average previous purchase day of 491 days ago.

For the sake of better readability, we will now order this RecencyCluster Sequence:

```
def                              order_cluster(cluster_field_name,
target_field_name,data,ascending):
  new_cluster_field_name = 'new_' + cluster_field_name
              df_new    =    data.groupby(cluster_field_name)
[target_field_name].mean().reset_index()
                                        df_new        =
df_new.sort_values(by=target_field_name,ascending=ascending).r
eset_index(drop=True)
  df_new['index'] = df_new.index
    df_final = pd.merge(data,df_new[[cluster_field_name,'index']],
on=cluster_field_name)
  df_final = df_final.drop([cluster_field_name],axis=1)
  df_final = df_final.rename(columns={"index":cluster_field_name})
  return df_final
CustUnique              =                order_cluster('RecencyCluster',
'Recency',CustUnique,False)
CustUnique.groupby('RecencyCluster')['Recency'].describe()
```

	count	mean	std	min	25%	50%	75%	max
RecencyCluster								
0	3.0	979.000000	72.794231	896.0	952.5	1009.0	1020.5	1032.0
1	2.0	491.000000	8.485281	485.0	488.0	491.0	494.0	497.0
2	30.0	23.366667	38.534788	0.0	1.0	10.0	25.0	168.0

Now we are using a similar clustering approach, this time for **Frequency**:

Frequency = data.groupby('Customer').SalesDate.count().reset_index()
Frequency.columns = ['Customer','Frequency']
Frequency.head()

	Customer	Frequency
0	0	46
1	1	176
2	2	7662
3	3	86
4	4	4164

We add frequency to recency using merge function:

CustUnique = pd.merge(CustUnique, Frequency, on='Customer')
CustUnique.head()

	Customer	Recency	RecencyCluster	Frequency
0	0	39	2	46
1	1	10	2	176
2	3	21	2	86
3	4	2	2	4164
4	5	28	2	437

And we also cluster frequency:

```python
CustUnique.Frequency.describe()
plot_data = [
  go.Histogram(
    x=CustUnique.['Frequency']
  )
]
plot_layout = go.Layout(
    title='Frequency'
  )
fig = go.Figure(data=plot_data, layout=plot_layout)
pyoff.iplot(fig)
```

```python
import warnings
warnings.filterwarnings("ignore")
import matplotlib.pyplot as plt
from sklearn.cluster import KMeans
inertia={}
Frequency = CustUnique[['Frequency']]
for k in range(1, 10):
  kmeans = KMeans(n_clusters=k, max_iter=1000).fit(Frequency)
  Frequency["clusters"] = kmeans.labels_
  inertia[k] = kmeans.inertia_
plt.figure(figsize=(10, 6))
plt.plot(list(inertia.keys()), list(inertia.values()), marker='o')
plt.xlabel("Number of cluster", fontsize=16)
plt.ylabel("Inertia", fontsize=16)
plt.xticks(list(inertia.keys()))
plt.show()
```

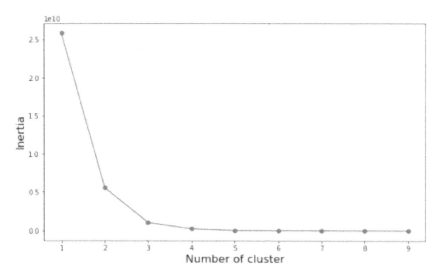

```
kmeans = KMeans(n_clusters=4)
kmeans.fit(CustUnique[['Frequency']])
CustUnique['FrequencyCluster']                              =
kmeans.predict(CustUnique[['Frequency']])
```

Unsupervised clustering has nothing to do with "AI that digests, understands and clusters data having the right expert knowledge at one`s disposal". There is no absolute wrong or right in any clustering method. It depends on the circumstances: maybe our salesforce will tell us that 5 clusters make more sense due to our company`s hierarchical structure, etc. ML can only give us a best guess, relying on data without domain knowledge. In the best case, clustering can lead to interesting questions that can help the company save or earn money. Unsupervised clustering is a beneficial approach to systematically grouping the data and finding extraordinary data points.

Why do we cluster the customers? We want to group them for an aligned "salesforce penetration". We want to group our customers into similar groups for our recommendation later. Or maybe we only want to compare customers with similar spending habits. If customers are grouped correctly, that would mean that each customer of a specified cluster should be dealt with similarly. For instance, the high cluster does not need an extra discount since we believe they will order anyway. Only if the predicted order is outstanding can the salesforce undertake some countermeasures. How does that help our salesforce colleagues? Cluster High is the most vital cluster, and we should try to keep them stuck with us. We do not want to lose them to our competitors. With regards to Cluster Mid, we could try to increase the frequency. At the same time, we have to undertake a more detailed analysis of the Low Cluster: do we want to invest in these customers, trying to make them buy again or/and in higher frequency, or would that be just a waste of money?

CustUnique.groupby('FrequencyCluster')['Frequency'].describe()

FrequencyCluster	count	mean	std	min	25%	50%	75%	max
0	30.0	1429.733333	2701.605907	1.0	36.0	138.0	463.25	8771.0
1	1.0	150043.000000	NaN	150043.0	150043.0	150043.0	150043.00	150043.0
2	3.0	28884.666667	1639.314593	27276.0	28050.5	28825.0	29689.00	30553.0
3	1.0	61833.000000	NaN	61833.0	61833.0	61833.0	61833.00	61833.0

CustUnique = order_cluster('FrequencyCluster', 'Frequency',CustUnique,True)
CustUnique.head()

	Customer	Recency	RecencyCluster	Frequency	FrequencyCluster
0	0	39	2	46	0
1	1	10	2	176	0
2	3	21	2	86	0
3	4	2	2	4164	0
4	5	28	2	437	0

For **MonetaryValue,** I used SalesValue (Net Sales). This can be modified after salesforce`s feedback, e.g., replaced by a margin, cost of sales, etc:

```
data['NetSales'] = data['SalesValue']
NetSales = data.groupby('Customer').NetSales.sum().reset_index()
NetSales.head()
```

	Customer	NetSales
0	0	365063.03
1	1	524331.16
2	2	7974948.61
3	3	71220.01
4	4	6286328.77

```
NetSales.sort_values(by='NetSales', ascending=False)
```

	Customer	NetSales
30	31	3.895101e+08
29	30	3.433869e+08
8	8	8.903569e+07
24	25	7.936539e+07
20	20	1.944865e+07
21	21	1.608147e+07

```
CustUnique = pd.merge(CustUnique, NetSales, on='Customer')
CustUnique.NetSales.describe()
plot_data = [
  go.Histogram(
    x=CustUnique.['NetSales']
  )
]
plot_layout = go.Layout(
    title='Monetary Value'
  )
fig = go.Figure(data=plot_data, layout=plot_layout)
pyoff.iplot(fig)
```

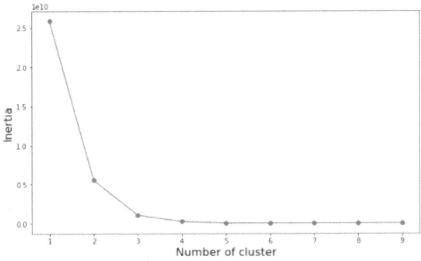

```
import warnings
warnings.filterwarnings("ignore")
import matplotlib.pyplot as plt
from sklearn.cluster import KMeans
inertia={}
tx_revenue = CustUnique[['NetSales']]
for k in range(1, 10):
    kmeans = KMeans(n_clusters=k, max_iter=1000).fit(Frequency)
    tx_revenue["clusters"] = kmeans.labels_
    inertia[k] = kmeans.inertia_
plt.figure(figsize=(10, 6))
plt.plot(list(inertia.keys()), list(inertia.values()), marker='o')
plt.xlabel("Number of cluster", fontsize=16)
plt.ylabel("Inertia", fontsize=16)
plt.xticks(list(inertia.keys()))
plt.show();
```

```
kmeans = KMeans(n_clusters=4)
kmeans.fit(CustUnique[['NetSales']])
CustUnique['NetSalesCluster']                                    =
kmeans.predict(CustUnique[['NetSales']])
CustUnique            =            order_cluster('NetSalesCluster',
'NetSales',CustUnique,True)
CustUnique.groupby('NetSalesCluster')['NetSales'].describe()
```

NetSalesCluster	count	mean	std	min	25%	50%	75%	max
0	31.0	3.633879e+06	5.440494e+06	3.304000e+02	7.990305e+04	5.243312e+05	5.031393e+06	1.944865e+07
1	2.0	8.420054e+07	6.837932e+06	7.936539e+07	8.178297e+07	8.420054e+07	8.661811e+07	8.903569e+07
2	1.0	3.433869e+08	NaN	3.433869e+08	3.433869e+08	3.433869e+08	3.433869e+08	3.433869e+08
3	1.0	3.895101e+08	NaN	3.895101e+08	3.895101e+08	3.895101e+08	3.895101e+08	3.895101e+08

Bringing it all together, we now have all three KPIs to calculate overall RFM clusters:

```
CustUnique.head()
```

	Customer	Recency	RecencyCluster	Frequency	FrequencyCluster	NetSales	NetSalesCluster
0	0	39	2	46	0	365063.03	0
1	1	10	2	176	0	524331.16	0
2	3	21	2	86	0	71220.01	0
3	4	2	2	4164	0	6286328.77	0
4	5	28	2	437	0	395756.34	0

```
CustUnique['OverallScore']   =   CustUnique['RecencyCluster']   +
CustUnique['FrequencyCluster'] + CustUnique['NetSalesCluster']
CustUnique.head()
```

	Customer	Recency	RecencyCluster	Frequency	FrequencyCluster	NetSales	NetSalesCluster	OverallScore
0	0	39	2	46	0	365063.03	0	2
1	1	10	2	176	0	524331.16	0	2
2	3	21	2	86	0	71220.01	0	2
3	4	2	2	4164	0	6286328.77	0	2
4	5	28	2	437	0	395756.34	0	2

CustUnique.groupby('OverallScore')
['Recency','Frequency','NetSales'].mean()

	Recency	Frequency	NetSales
OverallScore			
0	979.00	2935.666667	3.811347e+06
1	491.00	65.500000	1.267742e+06
2	27.96	1358.160000	3.169283e+06
3	0.00	27276.000000	1.944865e+07
4	1.00	29689.000000	8.420054e+07
7	0.00	105938.000000	3.664485e+08

CustUnique.groupby('OverallScore')['Recency'].count()

```
OverallScore
0     3
1     2
2    25
3     1
4     2
7     2
Name: Recency, dtype: int64
```

Clustering and segmentation are often used interchangeably, but they are not. Segmentation is used to apply the results of clustering, as we do now:

CustUnique['Segment'] = 'High'
CustUnique.loc[CustUnique['OverallScore']<5,'Segment'] = 'Mid'
CustUnique.loc[CustUnique['OverallScore']<4,'Segment'] = 'Low'
CustUnique.head()

175

	Customer	Recency	RecencyCluster	Frequency	FrequencyCluster	NetSales	NetSalesCluster	OverallScore	Segment
0	0	39	2	46	0	365063.03	0	2	Low
1	1	10	2	176	0	524331.16	0	2	Low
2	3	21	2	86	0	71220.01	0	2	Low
3	4	2	2	4164	0	6286328.77	0	2	Low
4	5	28	2	437	0	395756.34	0	2	Low

CustUnique.groupby('Segment').Customer.count()/
CustUnique.Customer.count()

```
Segment
High    0.057143
Low     0.885714
Mid     0.057143
Name: Customer, dtype: float64
```

Let us plot the four dimensions (R,F,M, and Segment highlighted) to see how the result looks like:

#import plotly_express as px
import plotly.express as px
fig = px.scatter_3d(CustUnique, x='Recency', y='Frequency', z='NetSales',
        color='Segment')
fig.show()

# Recency vs Frequency
GraphTwoDim = CustUnique
plot_data = [
  go.Scatter(
    x=GraphTwoDim.query("Segment == 'Low'")['Frequency'],
    y=GraphTwoDim.query("Segment == 'Low'")['Recency'],

```python
            text=GraphTwoDim['Customer'], # tooltip for customercode low
            mode='markers',
            name='Low',
            marker= dict(size= 7,
              line= dict(width=1),
              color= 'blue',
              opacity= 0.8
              )
        ),
        go.Scatter(
        x=GraphTwoDim.query("Segment == 'Mid'")['Frequency'],
        y=GraphTwoDim.query("Segment == 'Mid'")['Recency'],
        text=GraphTwoDim['Customer'], # tooltip for customercode low
        mode='markers',
        name='Mid',
        marker= dict(size= 9,
          line= dict(width=1),
          color= 'green',
          opacity= 0.5
          )
        ),
        go.Scatter(
        x=GraphTwoDim.query("Segment == 'High'")['Frequency'],
        y=GraphTwoDim.query("Segment == 'High'")['Recency'],
        text=GraphTwoDim['Customer'], # tooltip for customercode low
        mode='markers',
        name='High',
        marker= dict(size= 11,
          line= dict(width=1),
          color= 'red',
          opacity= 0.9
          )
        ),
]
plot_layout = go.Layout(
        yaxis= {'title': "Recency"},
        xaxis= {'title': "Frequency"},
        title='Segments'
```

```
    )
fig = go.Figure(data=plot_data, layout=plot_layout)
pyoff.iplot(fig)
```

```
# Recency vs NetSales
GraphTwoDim = CustUnique
plot_data = [
  go.Scatter(
    x=GraphTwoDim.query("Segment == 'Low'")['NetSales'],
    y=GraphTwoDim.query("Segment == 'Low'")['Recency'],
    text=GraphTwoDim['Customer'], # tooltip for customercode low
    mode='markers',
    name='Low',
    marker= dict(size= 7,
      line= dict(width=1),
      color= 'blue',
      opacity= 0.8
      )
),
    go.Scatter(
    x=GraphTwoDim.query("Segment == 'Mid'")['NetSales'],
    y=GraphTwoDim.query("Segment == 'Mid'")['Recency'],
    text=GraphTwoDim['Customer'], # tooltip for customercode low
    mode='markers',
    name='Mid',
    marker= dict(size= 9,
      line= dict(width=1),
```

```
        color= 'green',
        opacity= 0.5
        )
    ),
        go.Scatter(
        x=GraphTwoDim.query("Segment == 'High'")['NetSales'],
        y=GraphTwoDim.query("Segment == 'High'")['Recency'],
        text=GraphTwoDim['Customer'], # tooltip for customercode low
        mode='markers',
        name='High',
        marker= dict(size= 11,
            line= dict(width=1),
            color= 'red',
            opacity= 0.9
            )
    ),
]
plot_layout = go.Layout(
        yaxis= {'title': "Recency"},
        xaxis= {'title': "NetSales"},
        title='Segments'
    )
fig = go.Figure(data=plot_data, layout=plot_layout)
pyoff.iplot(fig)
```

Frequency vs NetSales

```python
GraphTwoDim = CustUnique
plot_data = [
  go.Scatter(
    x=GraphTwoDim.query("Segment == 'Low'")['NetSales'],
    y=GraphTwoDim.query("Segment == 'Low'")['Frequency'],
    text=GraphTwoDim['Customer'], # tooltip for customercode low
    mode='markers',
    name='Low',
    marker= dict(size= 7,
      line= dict(width=1),
      color= 'blue',
      opacity= 0.8
      )
  ),
    go.Scatter(
    x=GraphTwoDim.query("Segment == 'Mid'")['NetSales'],
    y=GraphTwoDim.query("Segment == 'Mid'")['Frequency'],
    text=GraphTwoDim['Customer'], # tooltip for customercode mid
    mode='markers',
    name='Mid',
    marker= dict(size= 9,
      line= dict(width=1),
      color= 'green',
      opacity= 0.5
      )
  ),
    go.Scatter(
    x=GraphTwoDim.query("Segment == 'High'")['NetSales'],
    y=GraphTwoDim.query("Segment == 'High'")['Frequency'],
      text=GraphTwoDim['Customer'], # tooltip for customercode high
    mode='markers',
    name='High',
    marker= dict(size= 11,
      line= dict(width=1),
      color= 'red',
      opacity= 0.9
      )
```

180

```
    ),
]
plot_layout = go.Layout(
    yaxis= {'title': "Frequency"},
    xaxis= {'title': "NetSales"},
    title='Segments'
)
fig = go.Figure(data=plot_data, layout=plot_layout)
pyoff.iplot(fig)
```

```
# Frequency vs Recency
GraphTwoDim = CustUnique
plot_data = [
  go.Scatter(
    x=GraphTwoDim.query("Segment == 'Low'")['Recency'],
    y=GraphTwoDim.query("Segment == 'Low'")['Frequency'],
    mode='markers',
    text=GraphTwoDim['Customer'], # tooltip for customercode low
    name='Low',
    marker= dict(size= 7,
      line= dict(width=1),
      color= 'blue',
      opacity= 0.8
      )
  ),
    go.Scatter(
    x=GraphTwoDim.query("Segment == 'Mid'")['Recency'],
    y=GraphTwoDim.query("Segment == 'Mid'")['Frequency'],
```

```
      mode='markers',
      text=GraphTwoDim['Customer'], # tooltip for customercode mid
      name='Mid',
      marker= dict(size= 9,
        line= dict(width=1),
        color= 'green',
        opacity= 0.5
        )
  ),
      go.Scatter(
      x=GraphTwoDim.query("Segment == 'High'")['Recency'],
      y=GraphTwoDim.query("Segment == 'High'")['Frequency'],
      mode='markers',
         text=GraphTwoDim['Customer'], # tooltip for customercode
high
      name='High',
      marker= dict(size= 11,
        line= dict(width=1),
        color= 'red',
        opacity= 0.9
        )
  ),
]
plot_layout = go.Layout(
    yaxis= {'title': "Frequency"},
    xaxis= {'title': "Recency"},
    title='Segments'
  )
fig = go.Figure(data=plot_data, layout=plot_layout)
pyoff.iplot(fig)
```

GraphTwoDim.head()

	Customer	Recency	RecencyCluster	Frequency	FrequencyCluster	NetSales	NetSalesCluster	OverallScore	Segment
0	0	39	2	46	0	365063.03	0	2	Low
1	1	10	2	176	0	524331.16	0	2	Low
2	3	21	2	86	0	71220.01	0	2	Low
3	4	2	2	4164	0	6286328.77	0	2	Low
4	5	28	2	437	0	395756.34	0	2	Low

Often, numeric features can vary together so that the variation in one feature will be duplicated by variation in another. **Principal components analysis** (PCA) is a way to discover any covariance. PCA combines multiple features into a smaller set of features, which are weighted linear combinations of the original set. The aim is to let a smaller feature space explain most of the variability of the complete original feature space. We will reduce four dimensions to two (pc1 and pc2).

```
from sklearn.decomposition import PCA
pca = PCA(n_components=2)
X = CustUnique[['RecencyCluster','FrequencyCluster','NetSalesCluster']]
principalComponents = pca.fit_transform(X)
principalDf = pd.DataFrame(data = principalComponents
        , columns = ['principal component 1', 'principal component 2'])
principalDf.head()
```

	principal component 1	principal component 2
0	-0.261465	-0.275183
1	-0.261465	-0.275183
2	-0.261465	-0.275183
3	-0.261465	-0.275183
4	-0.261465	-0.275183

MergedPcaDf = pd.concat([principalDf, CustUnique[['Segment']]], axis = 1) #OverallScore or Segment
MergedPcaDf.head()

	principal component 1	principal component 2	Segment
0	-0.261465	-0.275183	Low
1	-0.261465	-0.275183	Low
2	-0.261465	-0.275183	Low
3	-0.261465	-0.275183	Low
4	-0.261465	-0.275183	Low

```
fig = plt.figure(figsize = (8,8))
ax = fig.add_subplot(1,1,1)
ax.set_xlabel('Principal Component 1', fontsize = 15)
ax.set_ylabel('Principal Component 2', fontsize = 15)
ax.set_title('2 component PCA', fontsize = 20)
targets = ['Low','Mid','High']#targets = ['Low','Mid','High']#targets = ['1','2','3','4','5','8']
colors = ['r', 'g', 'b','c', 'm', 'y']
for target, color in zip(targets,colors):
  indicesToKeep = MergedPcaDf['Segment'] == target
  ax.scatter(MergedPcaDf.loc[indicesToKeep, 'principal component
```

1']

    , MergedPcaDf.loc[indicesToKeep, 'principal component 2']

    , c = color

    , s = 50)

ax.legend(targets)

ax.grid()

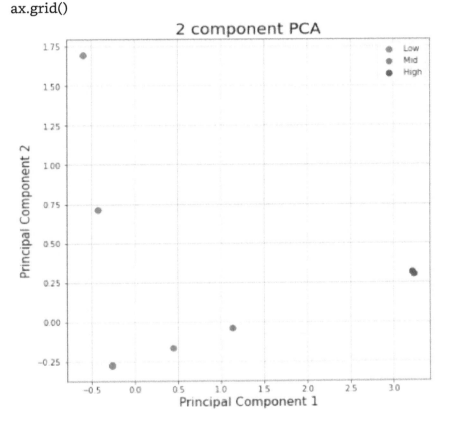

The explained variance (pca.explained_variance_ratio_) tells you how much information (variance) can be attributed to each principal component. This is important as while you can convert four-dimensional space to 2-dimensional space, you lose some of the variance (information) when you do this. Using the attribute explained_variance_ratio_, you can see that the first principal component contains 66% of the variance, and the second principal component includes 29% of the variance. Together, the two components contain 95% of the information. One of PCA's most essential applications is speeding up machine learning algorithms.

```
# checking the accuracy on our logistic regression
from numpy import mean
from numpy import std
from sklearn.datasets import make_classification
from sklearn.model_selection import cross_val_score
from sklearn.model_selection import RepeatedStratifiedKFold
from sklearn.pipeline import Pipeline
from sklearn.decomposition import PCA
from sklearn.linear_model import LogisticRegression
# define dataset
X, y = CustUnique[['RecencyCluster','FrequencyCluster','NetSalesCluster','NetSales','Recency','Frequency']],CustUnique.OverallScore
# define the pipeline
steps = [('pca', PCA(n_components=2)), ('m', LogisticRegression())]# reducing 3 features to 2
model = Pipeline(steps=steps)
# evaluate model
cv = RepeatedStratifiedKFold(n_splits=15, n_repeats=3, random_state=1)
n_scores = cross_val_score(model, X, y, scoring='accuracy', cv=cv, n_jobs=-1, error_score='raise')
# report performance
print('Accuracy: %.2f (%.2f)' % (mean(n_scores), std(n_scores)))
Accuracy: 0.72 (0.20)
# now making predictions with our PCA model
from sklearn.datasets import make_classification
from sklearn.pipeline import Pipeline
from sklearn.decomposition import PCA
from sklearn.linear_model import LogisticRegression
# define dataset
X, y = CustUnique[['RecencyCluster','FrequencyCluster','NetSalesCluster']]
```

```
,CustUnique.OverallScore # OverallScore vs Segment
# define the model
steps = [('pca', PCA(n_components=2)), ('m', LogisticRegression())]
model = Pipeline(steps=steps)
# fit the model on the whole dataset
model.fit(X, y)
# make a single prediction
#A new row of data with 3 columns is provided and is automatically
transformed to 2 components and fed to the logistic regression
model in order to predict the class label.
row = [[2,1,1]]
yhat = model.predict(row)
print('Predicted Class: %d' % yhat[0])
Predicted Class: 2
```

```
# After successfully reducing features with PCA, we will now
feature engineer even more to see if this improves our prediction
from datetime import datetime, timedelta,date
Past6M   =   data[(data.SalesDate   <   datetime   (2018,9,1))   &
(data.SalesDate >= datetime (2018,3,1))].reset_index(drop=True)
FirstPurchInMostCurrent3M          =          data[(data.SalesDate
>=      datetime(2018,9,1))     &      (data.SalesDate      <
datetime(2018,12,1))].reset_index(drop=True)
CustUnique.head()
```

	Customer	Recency	RecencyCluster	Frequency	FrequencyCluster	NetSales	NetSalesCluster	OverallScore	Segment
0	0	39	2	46	0	365063.03	0	2	Low
1	1	10	2	176	0	524331.16	0	2	Low
2	3	21	2	86	0	71220.01	0	2	Low
3	4	2	2	4164	0	6286328.77	0	2	Low
4	5	28	2	437	0	395756.34	0	2	Low

```
NextSales   =   data[(data.SalesDate   >=   datetime(2018,9,1))   &
(data.SalesDate < datetime(2018,12,1))].reset_index(drop=True)
```

Predict Customer`s next Purchase Date

We aim to predict the Customer's next purchase date based on
the Customer's past purchases. Suppose we estimate that the

customer purchases next week anyway. There is no need for particular actions (like events, discounts, etc). If that Customer has not purchased it in the predicted week, the salesforce might want to start specific treatments for that Customer afterward. So we calculate the difference for three successive purchase dates (if there are any; otherwise, NotaNumber NaN) per Customer (if the customer purchases >1 on the very same day, this gets de-duplicated). We can calculate the average and standard deviation for the differences in days between purchase dates and enrich these data points with our RFM scores.

```
#now adding more features
#create a dataframe with customer and first purchase date in
NextSales
NextSales_first_purchase                              =
NextSales.groupby('Customer').SalesDate.min().reset_index()
NextSales_first_purchase.columns                      =
['Customer','MinPurchaseDate']
#create a dataframe with customer and last purchase date in
FirstPurchInMostCurrent3M
LastSales                                             =
FirstPurchInMostCurrent3M.groupby('Customer').SalesDate.max().
reset_index()
LastSales.columns = ['Customer','MaxPurchaseDate']
#merge two dataframes
NextLastSales                                         =
pd.merge(LastSales,NextSales_first_purchase,on='Customer',how='
left')
#calculate the time difference in days:
NextLastSales['NextPurchaseDay']                      =
(NextLastSales['MaxPurchaseDate']                     -
NextLastSales['MinPurchaseDate']).dt.days
#merge with CustUnique
CustUnique              =              pd.merge(CustUnique,
```

NextLastSales[['Customer','NextPurchaseDay']],on='Customer',how
='left')
CustUnique.head()

	Customer	Recency	RecencyCluster	Frequency	FrequencyCluster	NetSales	NetSalesCluster	OverallScore	Segment	NextPurchaseDay
0	0	39	2	46	0	365063.03	0	2	Low	61.0
1	1	10	2	176	0	524331.16	0	2	Low	46.0
2	3	21	2	86	0	71220.01	0	2	Low	33.0
3	4	2	2	4164	0	6286328.77	0	2	Low	84.0
4	5	28	2	437	0	395756.34	0	2	Low	52.0

#create a dataframe with Customer and Purchase Date
FirstPurchInMostCurrent3MOrderedDaily   =
FirstPurchInMostCurrent3M[['Customer','SalesDate']]
#convert Invoice Datetime to day
FirstPurchInMostCurrent3MOrderedDaily['SalesDate']   =
FirstPurchInMostCurrent3M['SalesDate'].dt.date
FirstPurchInMostCurrent3MOrderedDaily   =
FirstPurchInMostCurrent3MOrderedDaily.sort_values(['Customer','
SalesDate'])
#drop duplicates
FirstPurchInMostCurrent3MOrderedDaily   =
FirstPurchInMostCurrent3MOrderedDaily.drop_duplicates(subset=
['Customer','SalesDate'],keep='first')
#shifting last 3 purchase dates
FirstPurchInMostCurrent3MOrderedDaily['PrevInvoiceDate']   =
FirstPurchInMostCurrent3MOrderedDaily.groupby('Customer')
['SalesDate'].shift(1)
FirstPurchInMostCurrent3MOrderedDaily['T2InvoiceDate']   =
FirstPurchInMostCurrent3MOrderedDaily.groupby('Customer')
['SalesDate'].shift(2)
FirstPurchInMostCurrent3MOrderedDaily['T3InvoiceDate']   =
FirstPurchInMostCurrent3MOrderedDaily.groupby('Customer')
['SalesDate'].shift(3)
FirstPurchInMostCurrent3MOrderedDaily.head()

	Customer	SalesDate	PrevInvoiceDate	T2InvoiceDate	T3InvoiceDate
3	0	2018-09-21	NaN	NaN	NaN
0	0	2018-09-28	2018-09-21	NaN	NaN
932	0	2018-10-30	2018-09-28	2018-09-21	NaN
2	0	2018-11-21	2018-10-30	2018-09-28	2018-09-21
1038	1	2018-10-11	NaN	NaN	NaN

FirstPurchInMostCurrent3MOrderedDaily['DayDiff']   =
(FirstPurchInMostCurrent3MOrderedDaily['SalesDate']   -
FirstPurchInMostCurrent3MOrderedDaily['PrevInvoiceDate']).dt.da
ys
FirstPurchInMostCurrent3MOrderedDaily['DayDiff2']   =
(FirstPurchInMostCurrent3MOrderedDaily['SalesDate']   -
FirstPurchInMostCurrent3MOrderedDaily['T2InvoiceDate']).dt.days
FirstPurchInMostCurrent3MOrderedDaily['DayDiff3']   =
(FirstPurchInMostCurrent3MOrderedDaily['SalesDate']   -
FirstPurchInMostCurrent3MOrderedDaily['T3InvoiceDate']).dt.days
FirstPurchInMostCurrent3MOrderedDaily.head()

	Customer	SalesDate	PrevInvoiceDate	T2InvoiceDate	T3InvoiceDate	DayDiff	DayDiff2	DayDiff3
3	0	2018-09-21	NaN	NaN	NaN	NaN	NaN	NaN
0	0	2018-09-28	2018-09-21	NaN	NaN	7.0	NaN	NaN
932	0	2018-10-30	2018-09-28	2018-09-21	NaN	32.0	39.0	NaN
2	0	2018-11-21	2018-10-30	2018-09-28	2018-09-21	22.0	54.0	61.0
1038	1	2018-10-11	NaN	NaN	NaN	NaN	NaN	NaN

FirstPurchInMostCurrent3MOrderedDailyDayDiff   =
FirstPurchInMostCurrent3MOrderedDaily.groupby('Customer').agg
({'DayDiff': ['mean','std']}).reset_index()
FirstPurchInMostCurrent3MOrderedDailyDayDiff.columns   =
['Customer', 'DayDiffMean','DayDiffStd']
FirstPurchInMostCurrent3MOrderedDaily_last   =
FirstPurchInMostCurrent3MOrderedDaily.drop_duplicates(subset=
['Customer'],keep='last')
FirstPurchInMostCurrent3MOrderedDaily_last   =
FirstPurchInMostCurrent3MOrderedDaily_last.dropna()
FirstPurchInMostCurrent3MOrderedDaily_last   =
pd.merge(FirstPurchInMostCurrent3MOrderedDaily_last,

FirstPurchInMostCurrent3MOrderedDailyDayDiff, on='Customer')
CustUnique   =   pd.merge(CustUnique,
FirstPurchInMostCurrent3MOrderedDaily_last[['Customer','DayDi
ff','DayDiff2','DayDiff3','DayDiffMean','DayDiffStd']], on='Customer')
NextPurchaseClass = CustUnique.copy()
NextPurchaseClass = pd.get_dummies(NextPurchaseClass)
CustUnique.head()

Customer	Recency	RecencyCluster	Frequency	FrequencyCluster	NetSales	NetSalesCluster	OverallScore	Segment	NextPurchaseDay	DayDiff	DayDiff2	DayDiff3	DayDiffMean	DayDiffStd
0	5	3	2	46	8	26.0061.03	0	2	Low	61.0	21.0	34.0	61.0	20.333333	12.983057
1	4	2	2	4164	8	9266328.77	0	2	Low	34.0	7.2	14.0	21.0	7.636784	4.653444
2	5	28	2	437	8	39575634	0	2	Low	52.0	14.0	38.0	52.0	17.333333	5.775502
3	7	5	2	4637	8	7512398.67	0	2	Low	84.5	7.0	14.0	21.0	7.200000	0.000000
4	12	7	2	7027	8	14279486.38	0	2	Low	84.0	7.0	11.0	14.0	7.000000	2.993699

NextPurchaseClass['NextPurchaseDayRange'] = 8
NextPurchaseClass.loc[NextPurchaseClass.NextPurchaseDay<88,'N
extPurchaseDayRange'] = 7
NextPurchaseClass.loc[NextPurchaseClass.NextPurchaseDay<86,'N
extPurchaseDayRange'] = 6
NextPurchaseClass.loc[NextPurchaseClass.NextPurchaseDay<84,'N
extPurchaseDayRange'] = 5
NextPurchaseClass.loc[NextPurchaseClass.NextPurchaseDay<82,'N
extPurchaseDayRange'] = 4
NextPurchaseClass.loc[NextPurchaseClass.NextPurchaseDay<80,'N
extPurchaseDayRange'] = 3
NextPurchaseClass.loc[NextPurchaseClass.NextPurchaseDay<78,'N
extPurchaseDayRange'] = 2
NextPurchaseClass.loc[NextPurchaseClass.NextPurchaseDay<76,'N
extPurchaseDayRange'] = 1
NextPurchaseClass.loc[NextPurchaseClass.NextPurchaseDay<74,'N
extPurchaseDayRange'] = 0
NextPurchaseClass.groupby('NextPurchaseDayRange').Customer.c
ount()/NextPurchaseClass.Customer.count()

```
NextPurchaseDayRange
0    0.294118
2    0.058824
6    0.352941
7    0.235294
8    0.058824
Name: Customer, dtype: float64
```

```python
import matplotlib.pyplot as plt
import seaborn as sns
corr = NextPurchaseClass[NextPurchaseClass.columns].corr()
plt.figure(figsize = (30,20))
sns.heatmap(corr, annot = True, linewidths=0.2, fmt=".2f")
```

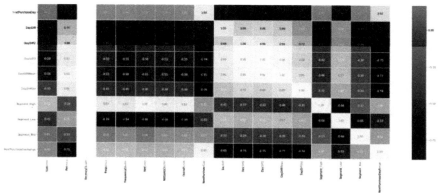

```python
corr_matrix=NextPurchaseClass.corr()
corr_matrix['NextPurchaseDayRange'].sort_values(ascending=False)
```

```
NextPurchaseDayRange      1.000000
NextPurchaseDay           0.923261
FrequencyCluster          0.550071
OverallScore              0.525936
Frequency                 0.520825
NetSalesCluster           0.469354
NetSales                  0.467209
Segment_High              0.377079
Segment_Mid               0.317169
Customer                  0.202176
Segment_Low              -0.527319
DayDiff                  -0.650556
Recency                  -0.707652
DayDiffStd               -0.742435
DayDiff3                 -0.746830
DayDiff2                 -0.759833
DayDiffMean              -0.767868
RecencyCluster                 NaN
Name: NextPurchaseDayRange, dtype: float64
```

NextPurchaseClass.head()

```
import xgboost as xgb
from sklearn.model_selection import KFold, cross_val_score,
train_test_split
X, y
= NextPurchaseClass.drop('NextPurchaseDayRange',axis=1),
NextPurchaseClass.NextPurchaseDayRange
X_train, X_test, y_train, y_test = train_test_split(X, y,
test_size=0.2, random_state=44)
from sklearn.linear_model import LogisticRegression
from sklearn.naive_bayes import GaussianNB
from sklearn.ensemble import RandomForestClassifier
from sklearn.tree import DecisionTreeClassifier
from sklearn.svm import SVC
#create an array of models
models = []
models.append(("LR",LogisticRegression()))
models.append(("NB",GaussianNB()))
models.append(("RF",RandomForestClassifier()))
models.append(("SVC",SVC()))
models.append(("Dtree",DecisionTreeClassifier()))
#measure the accuracy
for name,model in models:
  kfold = KFold(n_splits=2, random_state=22)
    cv_result = cross_val_score(model,X_train,y_train, cv =
kfold,scoring = "accuracy")
  print(name, cv_result)
```

```
LR [0.14285714 0.        ]
NB [0.42857143 0.66666667]
RF [0.42857143 0.66666667]
SVC [0.28571429 0.33333333]
Dtree [0.42857143 0.5       ]
XGB [0.14285714 0.5       ]
```

Let us take a look at xgboost (extreme gradient boosting) in more
detail.

```
xgb_model = xgb.XGBClassifier().fit(X_train, y_train)
print('Accuracy of XGB classifier on training set: {:.2f}'
   .format(xgb_model.score(X_train, y_train)))
print('Accuracy of XGB classifier on test set: {:.2f}'
   .format(xgb_model.score(X_test[X_train.columns], y_test)))
```

```
Accuracy of XGB classifier on training set: 0.92
Accuracy of XGB classifier on test set: 0.75
```

We have already mentioned decision trees but have not yet defined them. I think now is an excellent moment to satisfy this obligation. A decision tree consists of a **root** node (starting node), **interior** nodes, and **leaf** nodes (ending nodes) connected by branches. Each non-leaf node (root and interior) represents a test to be carried out. The number of possible levels a feature can take determines the number of downward branches from a non-leaf node. Each of the leaf nodes specifies a predicted level of the target feature. Using a decision tree to indicate a query instance starts by testing the feature's value at the tree's root node. The result of this test determines which of the root node's children the process should descend to. These two steps are then repeated until the process reaches a leaf node at which a prediction can be made.

Much of the focus of ML is on developing the single most accurate prediction model possible for a given task. In contrast to that approach, we can also use **model ensembles** (like sklearn.ensemble) to create a set of models (instead of just using one model) and then make predictions by aggregating the outputs of these models. The idea behind ensemble methods is the assumption that many learners working together are more likely to fit more precisely than a single learner alone. Each model within the ensemble models will make predictions independently of the other models in the ensemble. Suppose the ensemble consists of many independent models. In that case, the overall achievement of the model can be very accurate even if the individual models in the ensemble perform only marginally better than random guessing. Ensemble models are defined as being built up on multiple different models from the same dataset by inducing each model using a different slice of the dataset. The other ensemble technique is based on aggregating the predictions of the various models. **Boosting** is one approach to set up ensembles that are prone to overfitting. The reason is that each new model added to an ensemble via boosting is biased to pay more attention to instances that previous models misclassified. To avoid overfitting, we will use hyperparameter tuning to balance overfitting with the accuracy and computational complexity. In contrast to **random forest**, which fits very deep trees, boosting usually fits shallow trees (including a penalty term on the number of parameters, also called **regularization).** This has the advantage of avoiding misleading interactions in the model from **noisy** data. **Cross-validation** (CV) is especially important for xgb due to the large amount of hyperparameter settings.

```
from sklearn.model_selection import GridSearchCV
param_test1 = {
'max_depth':range(3,10,2),
'min_child_weight':range(1,6,2)
}
gsearch1 = GridSearchCV(estimator = xgb.XGBClassifier(),
param_grid                        = param_test1,
scoring='accuracy',n_jobs=-1,iid=False, cv=2)
gsearch1.fit(X_train,y_train)
gsearch1.best_params_, gsearch1.best_score_
```
```
({'max_depth': 3, 'min_child_weight': 1}, 0.4642857142857143)
```

```
ltv_xgb_model         =         xgb.XGBClassifier(max_depth=5,
learning_rate=0.1,objective=
'multi:softprob',n_jobs=-1).fit(X_train, y_train)
print('Accuracy of XGB classifier on training set: {:.2f}'
    .format(ltv_xgb_model.score(X_train, y_train)))
print('Accuracy of XGB classifier on test set: {:.2f}'
        .format(ltv_xgb_model.score(X_test[X_train.columns],
y_test)))
```

```
Accuracy of XGB classifier on training set: 0.92
Accuracy of XGB classifier on test set: 0.75
```
We should remember the overall clusters:
```
NextPurchaseClass.groupby('NextPurchaseDayRange').Custome
r.count()/NextPurchaseClass.Customer.count()
```

```
NextPurchaseDayRange
0    0.294118
2    0.058824
6    0.352941
7    0.235294
8    0.058824
Name: Customer, dtype: float64
```

To be able to evaluate our results more meaningful:

```
from sklearn.metrics import classification_report
print (classification_report(y_test, y_pred))

              precision    recall  f1-score   support

           0       1.00      0.50      0.67         2
           6       0.50      1.00      0.67         1
           7       1.00      1.00      1.00         1

    accuracy                           0.75         4
   macro avg       0.83      0.83      0.78         4
weighted avg       0.88      0.75      0.75         4
```

Now that we have clustered the customers with regards to sales frequency, recency and monetary value we try to predict customers future sales.

2.3 SALES PREDICTION

We have analyzed past sales in detail using clustering and feature engineering techniques. Now we are looking forward to trying to predict how much we will sell in the future. We try to predict future sales based on past time series sales data. A time series is generally a data set collected through time. Estimating future sales is helpful in quite a few ways. First, we can see our prediction as a benchmark (similar to a budget or plan). Our predicted values are mathematically made up of past data, and we try to put the data`s patterns into a function. We can, therefore, describe our prediction as a value that should become real if nothing else changes. If we sell more than estimated, that could be due to salesforce actions like special marketing events, substantial discounts, etc. If we sell less, that could mean that our salesforce did not invent as much energy as they did for these items and customers in the past. In real life, many variables influence sales, making predicting time series tricky. But we are assuming that patterns that existed in the past will continue on into the future. However, we assume that patterns that existed in the past will continue. Real-life time series data are often not simple, but what else can we do? As we have already touched on in chapter 2.1, we know that time series is always about breaking down the past into any trend (moving in a specific direction), seasonal (repeating fluctuation or patterns at predictable intervals), and residual (autocorrelation and noise) parts. Autocorrelation means it correlates with a delayed copy of itself and is often called a lag. This is also called serial correlation (having memory as steps depend on previous ones). For instance, if we had high sales in a couple of consecutive days, we would most likely expect them to be high the next day in that sequence as well. By shifting the time series by an interval (lag), we can compute the correlation between the shifted series and the original.

Sales time series is very much different from, let`s say, experimental scientific data under laboratory conditions. Sales time series often include a lot of noise. ML models can only make predictions if any patterns can be spotted. Noise, by definition, does not include visible patterns and hence is unpredictable. That is why we will very unlikely see any model that can precisely predict sales data in the future. However, as mentioned, we can treat the prediction as a mathematical kind of status quo. So any deviations from that model against past sales could indicate questions like "Why did the market change?", "in what way did our salesforce change their efforts," etc.

First of all, we will bring the data (frame) into a "ready for our ML algorithms"-to use shape:

```python
import pandas as pd
df = pd.read_excel('/content/gdrive/My Drive/DDDDFolder/DDDD.xlsx',parse_dates=['SalesDate'])
df.head()
```

	SalesDate	SalesValue	SalesAmount	Customer	SalesTransactionID	SalesItem
0	2018-09-28	8280.0	10	0	0	0
1	2018-09-28	7452.0	10	0	0	0
2	2019-04-23	21114.0	30	0	1	0
3	2019-04-23	7038.0	10	0	1	1
4	2019-04-23	7000.0	2	0	1	2

2.3.1 BENCHMARK

The first model we will use is Seasonal Autoregressive Integrated Moving Average **(SARIMA),** a combination of simple models that can make up a complex model.

ARIMA consists of **(p,d,q)** coefficients.
p stands for the **autogression** (which is basically a linear regression).
d stands for the **integrated** (order of differencing): If we see a trend, then our data is not **stationary**. Stationary means there is no systematic change in the mean and variance of one section of a specific time window compared to another: the time series' behavior does not change over time, and there are no periodic fluctuations (variations). If our time series is not stationary, we must transform it using **differencing.** Differencing means to remove the trend and seasonality from the time series. So, instead of studying the time series itself, we study the difference between the value at a specific time and an earlier period (e.g., one year, day, month, etc). After we have differenced our data, we will no longer see a trend or seasonality. Forecasts on different time series finally just need to be added back to the value at a specific time minus the earlier period. We will use **Augmented Dicky-Fuller** (ADF) to check whether the time series is stationary (stationary means that mean and variance remain constant over time). Overall, differencing makes time series more predictable. The null hypothesis (H0) of ADF is that our time is not stationary, while the alternate hypothesis would indicate that the series is stationary. H0 is a statement about the population that is either believed to be true or used to put forth an argument unless it can be shown to be incorrect beyond a reasonable doubt.

q stands for **moving average**, a standard and straightforward forecasting method. The idea is to calculate the mean over a fixed period called an averaging window. This eliminates a lot of noise and gives us a curve roughly emulating the original series, but it does not anticipate any trend or seasonality. p and q values are estimated using **ACF** and **PACF** plots (see chapter 2.1: ACF plots autocorrelation coefficients at different lags in a **Correlogram**). The moving average (MA) method models the next step in the sequence as a linear function of the residual errors from a mean process at prior time steps. SARIMA also includes (P, D,Q,s) for the seasonal aspects.

```
#simple mean prediction as benchmark
import matplotlib.pyplot as plt
df3=df.drop(columns=[ 'SalesValue','Customer','SalesTransactionID','SalesItem'])
df3['SalesDate'] = pd.to_datetime(df3['SalesDate'])
df3 = df3.set_index('SalesDate')
daily_df = df3.resample('MS').sum()#D vs resample(ms); M monthhly vs D daily ws weekly w, M End of month, MS start of month
d_df = daily_df.reset_index().dropna()
d_df.columns = ['ds', 'y']
fig = plt.figure(facecolor='w', figsize=(20, 6))
plt.plot(d_df.ds, d_df.y)
```

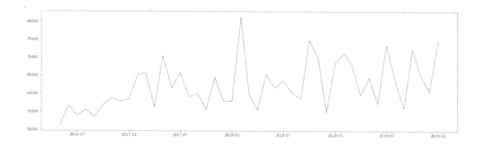

```python
import warnings
import itertools
import numpy as np
import matplotlib.pyplot as plt
warnings.filterwarnings("ignore")
plt.style.use('fivethirtyeight')
import pandas as pd
import statsmodels.api as sm
import matplotlib
matplotlib.rcParams['axes.labelsize'] = 14
matplotlib.rcParams['xtick.labelsize'] = 12
matplotlib.rcParams['ytick.labelsize'] = 12
matplotlib.rcParams['text.color'] = 'k'
import scipy as sp
p = d = q = range(0, 2)
pdq = list(itertools.product(p, d, q))
seasonal_pdq = [(x[0], x[1], x[2], 12) for x in list(itertools.product(p, d, q))]


warnings.filterwarnings("ignore") # specify to ignore warning messages
for param in pdq:
    for param_seasonal in seasonal_pdq:
        try:
            mod = sm.tsa.statespace.SARIMAX(daily_df,
                        order=param,
```

```
            seasonal_order=param_seasonal,

            enforce_stationarity=False,

            enforce_invertibility=False)

    results = mod.fit()

    print('ARIMA{}x{}12 - AIC:{}'.format(param, param_seasonal,
results.aic))

    except:

    continue
```

```
ARIMA(1, 1, 1)x(0, 0, 0, 12)12 - AIC:866.877208751924 1
ARIMA(1, 1, 1)x(0, 0, 1, 12)12 - AIC:2868.7577461288447
ARIMA(1, 1, 1)x(0, 1, 0, 12)12 - AIC:629.2507861992482
ARIMA(1, 1, 1)x(1, 0, 0, 12)12 - AIC:637.9720297324675
ARIMA(1, 1, 1)x(1, 0, 1, 12)12 - AIC:620.3624677433077
ARIMA(1, 1, 1)x(1, 1, 0, 12)12 - AIC:398.14889488761065
```

```
import statsmodels.api as sm
mod = sm.tsa.statespace.SARIMAX(daily_df,
                    order=(1, 1, 1),#lowest AIC, see results above
                    seasonal_order=(1, 1, 0, 12), #lowest AIC, see results above
```

AIC stands for Akaike information criterion, where a lower AIC indicates a better model. In general, the AIC likes to choose simple models with lower order. The AIC gives credit for models that reduce the error sum of squares while building in a penalty for models that introduce too many parameters.

```
import statsmodels.api as sm
mod = sm.tsa.statespace.SARIMAX(daily_df,
            order=(1, 1, 1),
            seasonal_order=(1, 1, 0, 12),
            enforce_stationarity=False,
            enforce_invertibility=False)
results = mod.fit()

pred = results.get_prediction(start=pd.to_datetime('2019-05-01'),
dynamic=False)
pred_ci = pred.conf_int()
ax = daily_df['2016':].plot(label='observed')
```

```
pred.predicted_mean.plot(ax=ax,    label='Prediction',    alpha=.7,
figsize=(14, 7))
ax.fill_between(pred_ci.index,
       pred_ci.iloc[:, 0],
       pred_ci.iloc[:, 1], color='k', alpha=.2)
ax.set_xlabel('Period')
ax.set_ylabel('Sales Quantity')
plt.legend()
plt.show()
```

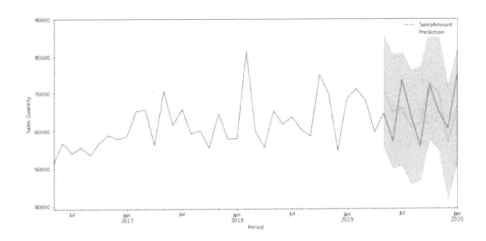

```
pred_uc = results.get_forecast(steps=12) #60 steps: 5 years (60
periods) forecast
pred_ci = pred_uc.conf_int()
ax = daily_df.plot(label='observed', figsize=(14, 7))
pred_uc.predicted_mean.plot(ax=ax, label='Forecast')
ax.fill_between(pred_ci.index,
       pred_ci.iloc[:, 0],
       pred_ci.iloc[:, 1], color='k', alpha=.25)
ax.set_xlabel('Period')
ax.set_ylabel('Sales Amount')
plt.legend()
plt.show()
```

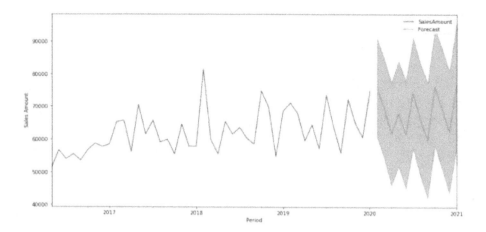

print (pred_uc.predicted_mean)

Enough talking the talking, now let's walk the walk.

Let us use our first supervised ML model to predict future sales quantity. We will not change data frame settings to make a transparent and fair comparison against the predicted mean model.

2.3.2 PROPHET SALES

Now, we will check another approach trying to predict future sales, namely Facebook`s Prophet. After importing the Prophet from the FbProphet library we will come to the first difference right away. This time, we have to create a df, which consists of y and s. This is how Prophet deals with df if we want to predict time series. This is because, in ML, we have to divide the data into features and labels. For time series, our feature effectively has several values in the series, with the label being the very next value in that sequence order.

```python
import pandas as pd
import matplotlib.pyplot as plt
import seaborn as sns
from fbprophet import Prophet
%matplotlib inline
data = pd.read_excel('/content/gdrive/My Drive/DDDDFolder/DDDD.xlsx')
df3=data.drop(columns=[                                   'Customer',
'SalesItem','SalesTransactionID','SalesValue'])
df3['SalesDate'] = pd.to_datetime(df3['SalesDate'])
df3 = df3.set_index('SalesDate')
daily_df = df3.resample('MS').sum()# M End of month, MS start of
month vs D daily vs weekly w; please note that Prophet is said to
work best for daily data!
d_df = daily_df.reset_index().dropna()
d_df.columns = ['ds', 'y']
d_df.head()
```

	ds	y
0	2016-05-01	51265
1	2016-06-01	56692
2	2016-07-01	53954
3	2016-08-01	55496
4	2016-09-01	53552

```
d_df.columns = ['ds', 'y']
fig = plt.figure(facecolor='w', figsize=(20, 6))
plt.plot(d_df.ds, d_df.y)
```

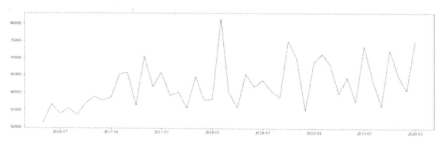

Then, as usual, we will instantiate the model by choosing a seasonality_mode and an interval_width and setting the amount of, e.g., months we want to predict via setting the variable for periods and frequency MS for month start. Now, we can simply plot actual and forecasted values by instantiating the model and plotting the forecast:

```
m                                                                    =
Prophet(seasonality_mode='additive',interval_width=0.95).fit(d_df
) #additive vs multiplicative seasonality, 95% confidence interval
future = m.make_future_dataframe(periods=12, freq='MS')# vs just
periods=365 --> which works well for weekly and daily
fcst = m.predict(future)
fig = m.plot(fcst)
```

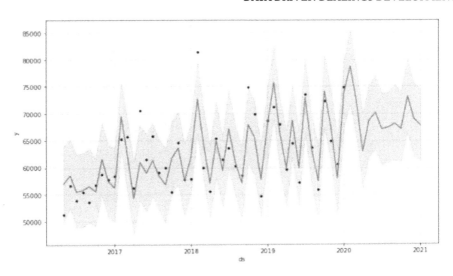

Doing the same, but this time dynamically:

```
from fbprophet.plot import plot_plotly
import plotly.offline as py
py.init_notebook_mode()
fig = plot_plotly(m,fcst)
#py.iplot(fig)
fig.show(renderer="colab")
```

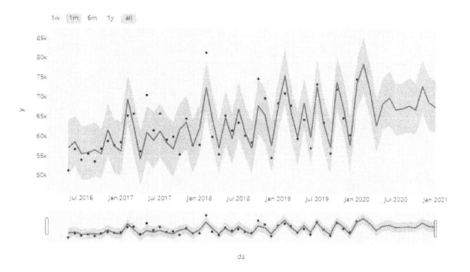

What is that graph trying to tell us? The blue line shows the forecasted sales quantities, which Prophet predicted while trying to fit a model with the lowest overall error on our actual data points. The black dots show the actual sales quantities in the past. The blue shade is the confidence interval, meaning that the model would estimate that the sales quantity must be within this range. We can see that we are facing the first sold quantity in April, which does not fit into the model`s confidence interval. Is that because our actual value is wrong, or is our model crap? Firstly, none of our past sales quantities are wrong. Our FIBU/CO colleagues checked and matched them with the official month`s end-closing values. So our model must be garbage, right? No, it is not that easy: our Prophet model has no intelligence behind the numbers; it is just mathematically and statistically trying to model our sales quantities.

With regard to the numbers, we could argue (without any domain knowledge background) that these data points look extraordinary so that they could be outliers. The question is: do we want our model also to be trained on these unique data points or not? As our sales colleagues are telling us, these data points belong to special political reasons in the sales countries (Russia was annexing the Krim, the USA shook the world with new tolls, so did China, etc.). However, since all our data points do not have any data transfer errors and simply display our real sales environment, we will not change any of our data. The models we are fitting will need to be trained on all sales data points, and the model that will be able also to include these extraordinary data points will win the job for us!

```
m = Prophet()
m.fit(d_df)
future     =   m.make_future_dataframe(periods=12,     freq='MS')
#periods=12, freq='MS' for monthly start month vs periods=365 for
daily and weekly
forecast = m.predict(future)
forecast[['ds', 'yhat', 'yhat_lower', 'yhat_upper']].tail()
```

	ds	yhat	yhat_lower	yhat_upper
52	2020-09-01	68090.916223	63757.455614	72411.834847
53	2020-10-01	67106.175174	62556.626432	71457.633473
54	2020-11-01	73151.416132	68513.837418	77599.592319
55	2020-12-01	69010.958622	64486.153217	73452.079938
56	2021-01-01	67792.183576	63118.598808	72586.785588

```
forecast[['ds', 'yhat', 'yhat_lower', 'yhat_upper']][-90:]
```

	ds	yhat	yhat_lower	yhat_upper
0	2016-05-01	57026.679801	52444.539581	61511.440148
1	2016-06-01	58512.795679	54157.647054	62868.320880
2	2016-07-01	55496.841697	50775.769696	60015.290445
3	2016-08-01	55797.470347	51512.879398	60209.742219

Adding a trend to our time series:

```
from datetime import datetime, timedelta
from fbprophet.plot import add_changepoints_to_plot #trend line
fig = m.plot(forecast)
a = add_changepoints_to_plot(fig.gca(), m, forecast) #trend line
```

```
datenow = datetime(2020, 1, 1)
dateend = datenow + timedelta(days=180)
datestart = dateend - timedelta(days=1600)
plt.xlim([datestart, dateend])
plt.title("Sales forecast", fontsize=20)
plt.xlabel("Period", fontsize=20)
plt.ylabel("Sales Amount", fontsize=20)
plt.axvline(datenow, color="k", linestyle=":")
plt.show()
```

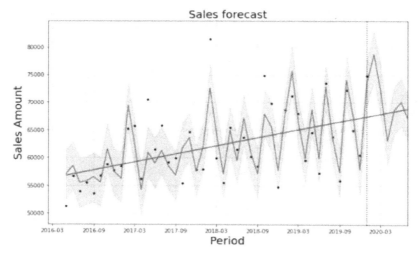

```
fig2 = m.plot_components(forecast)
```

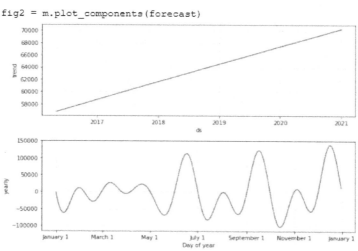

Prophet's prediction disaggregated into a trend, weekly (if we would have used daily time series), and yearly components. From this, the prediction is formed by a sum of the components, which are formed differently (e.g., the trend is linear).

```
from        fbprophet.diagnostics      import      cross_validation,
performance_metrics
df_cv = cross_validation(m, horizon='90 days')
#df_cv = cross_validation(m, initial='1095 days', period='30 days',
horizon = '60 days')#365 days = 1year
#do cross-validation to assess prediction performance on a horizon
of 60 days, starting with 1095 days of training data in
#the first cutoff and then making predictions every 30 days. This
corresponds to x total forecasts.
#initial: how many days for training
df_p = performance_metrics(df_cv)
df_p.head(5)
#mean squared error (MSE), root mean squared error (RMSE), mean
absolute error (MAE), mean absolute percent error (MAPE),
#and coverage of the yhat_lower and yhat_upper estimates.
#The performance_metrics utility can be used to compute some
useful statistics of the
#prediction performance (yhat, yhat_lower, and yhat_upper
compared to y), as a function of the distance from the cutoff
#(how far into the future the prediction was). The statistics
computed are mean squared error (MSE),
#root mean squared error (RMSE), mean absolute error (MAE), mean
absolute percent error (MAPE),
#and coverage of the yhat_lower and yhat_upper estimates. These
are computed on a rolling window of the predictions
#in df_cv after sorting by horizon (ds minus cutoff). By default 10%
of the predictions will be included in each window,
#but this can be changed with the rolling_window argument.
```

	horizon	mse	rmse	mae	mape	mdape	coverage
0	8 days	3.461766e+09	58836.774190	39335.545060	0.651165	0.399282	0.000000
1	9 days	7.215475e+08	26861.635818	17515.841867	0.294765	0.072338	0.166667
2	11 days	3.751801e+08	19369.567033	11167.581448	0.187853	0.072338	0.166667
3	13 days	2.108240e+07	4591.557167	4099.348131	0.068573	0.068230	0.333333

#do cross-validation to assess prediction performance on a horizon of 60 days, starting with 1095 days of training data in
#the first cutoff and then making predictions every 30 days. This corresponds to x total forecasts.
#initial: how many days for training
df_cv.head(20)
#cross-validation to assess prediction performance on a horizon of 60 days, starting with 1095 days/3years of training data in the first cutoff and then making predictions every 30 days. On this >3 year time series, this corresponds to ? total forecasts.
y is actual, yhat is predicted value

	ds	yhat	yhat_lower	yhat_upper	y	cutoff
0	2017-06-01	189553.190068	189553.190017	189553.190117	61501	2017-05-31
1	2017-07-01	105250.180530	105250.180396	105250.180654	65768	2017-05-31
2	2017-08-01	190067.319967	190067.319721	190067.320216	59127	2017-05-31

```
from fbprophet.plot import plot_cross_validation_metric
fig3 = plot_cross_validation_metric(df_cv, metric='mse')
```

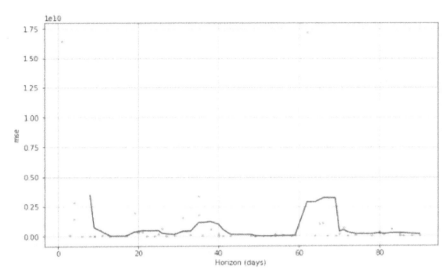

We can also **flag** the **detected anomalies** in the df directly:

```
def detect_anomalies(forecast):
    forecasted = forecast[['ds','trend', 'yhat', 'yhat_lower', 'yhat_upper',
'fact']].copy()
    #forecast['fact'] = df['y']
    forecasted['anomaly'] = 0
        forecasted.loc[forecasted['fact'] > forecasted['yhat_upper'],
'anomaly'] = 1
        forecasted.loc[forecasted['fact'] < forecasted['yhat_lower'],
'anomaly'] = -1
    #anomaly importances
    forecasted['importance'] = 0
    forecasted.loc[forecasted['anomaly'] ==1, 'importance'] = \
        (forecasted['fact'] - forecasted['yhat_upper'])/forecast['fact']
    forecasted.loc[forecasted['anomaly'] ==-1, 'importance'] = \
        (forecasted['yhat_lower'] - forecasted['fact'])/forecast['fact']
    return forecasted
```

The model should be re-trained when new data becomes available. There is no point in re-training the model if the data is unchanged. Instead, we can **save** and use the model again to call the predict function. We can use **pickle** for that:

```
import pickle
with open('forecast_model.pckl', 'wb') as fout:
    pickle.dump(m, fout)
with open('forecast_model.pckl', 'rb') as fin:
    m2 = pickle.load(fin)
```

Until now, we have forecasted all items for all customers. We had to filter beforehand to predict a specific customer and sales item combination. Let us now see how we can do this in one stroke on an overall level so we can forecast per SalesItem in one loop, exporting the results of all individual SalesItems forecasts into one Excel file:

```
import pandas as pd
data = pd.read_excel('/content/gdrive/My Drive/DDDDFolder/DDDD.xlsx')
from fbprophet import Prophet
#If you should receive an error "future is not defined" when running with your data, your SalesDate column in Excel might not be formatted as date.
gData = data.groupby(['SalesItem', 'SalesDate'])['SalesAmount'].sum()
gData = gData.to_frame().reset_index()
itemlist = gData.SalesItem.unique()
m = Prophet()
fcst_all = pd.DataFrame() # store all forecasts here
for x in itemlist:
    temp = gData[gData.SalesItem == x]
    temp = temp.drop(columns=[ 'SalesItem'])
```

```
temp['SalesDate'] = pd.to_datetime(temp['SalesDate'])
temp = temp.set_index('SalesDate')
d_df = temp.resample('MS').sum()
d_df = d_df.reset_index().dropna()
d_df.columns = ['ds', 'y']
try:
                                                        m       =
Prophet(seasonality_mode='additive',interval_width=0.95).fit(d_df
)
    future = m.make_future_dataframe(periods=12, freq='MS')
except ValueError:
    pass
fcst = m.predict(future)
fcst['Artikel'] = x
fcst['Fact'] = d_df['y'].reset_index(drop = True)
fcst_all = pd.concat((fcst_all, fcst))
print(x)
fcst_all.to_excel('ProphetFc.xlsx', index=False)
```

Here you go: all sales items have been individually forecasted, and all results have been exported to an Excel file called ProphetFc. If the column "Fact" is flagged with "y", this data row represents an actual value. If not, it is a predicted value.

2.3.3 LONG SHORT-TERM MEMORY

Finally, we will try to predict future sales with the Long Short-term Memory **(LSTM)** method, using a **deep learning** technique (Tensorflow/ Keras). Sales prediction is used as another benchmark value (besides being a good sidekick for budget planning) for salesforce. In other words, predicting future sales from past values can display business as usual if there are no "strategy salesforce changes". Therefore, predicted sales can also be used to calculate incremental value due to salesforce actions like events, discounts, etc.

Before we can feed and fire any **neurons**, we have to first prepare our data as usual:

```
import pandas as pd
data = pd.read_excel('/content/gdrive/My Drive/DDDDFolder/DDDD.xlsx',parse_dates=['SalesDate'])
df3=data.drop(columns=['Customer','SalesItem','SalesTransactionID','SalesValue'])
df3['SalesDate'] = pd.to_datetime(df3['SalesDate'])
df3['SalesDate'] = pd.to_datetime(df3['SalesDate'])
df3 = df3.set_index('SalesDate')
daily_df = df3.resample('M').sum()#D
df4 = daily_df.reset_index().dropna()
```

```
df4 = df4.set_index('SalesDate')
df4.head()
```

```
           SalesAmount
SalesDate
2016-05-31     51265
2016-06-30     56692
2016-07-31     53954
2016-08-31     55496
2016-09-30     53552
```

```
import numpy as np
from pandas.tseries.offsets import DateOffset
from sklearn.preprocessing import MinMaxScaler
import tensorflow as tf
from tensorflow import keras
from tensorflow.keras.preprocessing.sequence import
TimeseriesGenerator
from tensorflow.keras.models import Sequential
from tensorflow.keras.layers import Dense
from tensorflow.keras.layers import LSTM
from tensorflow.keras.layers import Dropout
import warnings
warnings.filterwarnings("ignore")
```

TensorFlow and Keras are the most widely used and known open-source ML tools. Keras is a higher-level API for TensorFlow that is very user-friendly. Google has even created special hardware (Tensor Processing Units) to improve TensorFlow further.

```
train = df4
scaler = MinMaxScaler()
scaler.fit(train)
train = scaler.transform(train)
n_input = 12
n_features = 1
generator = TimeseriesGenerator(train, train, length=n_input,
```

```
batch_size=6)
model = Sequential()
model.add(LSTM(200,    activation='relu',    input_shape=(n_input,
n_features)))
```
Rectified Linear Unit (relu) takes the input value and puts it in the range of 0 to infinity.
```
model.add(Dropout(0.15))
```
Dropout layers control overfitting. Dropout is used during the training phase and randomly drops out a set of 15% of the model's neurons.
```
model.add(Dense(1))
optimizer = keras.optimizers.Adam(lr=0.001)
```
The optimizer defines how the weights of the model are adjusted.
```
model.compile(optimizer=optimizer, loss='mse')
history = model.fit_generator(generator,epochs=800,verbose=1)
```

The model displays a log while it is running:

```
WARNING:tensorflow:From <ipython-input-43-634d81ca8db3>:32: Model.fit_generator (from tensorflow.python.keras
Instructions for updating:
Please use Model.fit, which supports generators.
Epoch 1/800
6/6 [==============================] - 0s 17ms/step - loss: 0.2032
Epoch 2/800
6/6 [==============================] - 0s 15ms/step - loss: 0.1038
Epoch 3/800
6/6 [==============================] - 0s 17ms/step - loss: 0.0533
```

```
import plotly.offline as pyoff
import plotly.graph_objs as go
hist = pd.DataFrame(history.history)
hist['epoch'] = history.epoch
plot_data = [
  go.Scatter(
    x=hist['epoch'],
    y=hist['loss'],
    name='loss'
  )
]
plot_layout = go.Layout(
    title='Training loss'
```

```
    )
fig = go.Figure(data=plot_data, layout=plot_layout)
#pyoff.iplot(fig)
fig.show(renderer="colab")
```

```
pred_list = []
batch = train[-n_input:].reshape((1, n_input, n_features))
for i in range(n_input):
    pred_list.append(model.predict(batch)[0])
    batch = np.append(batch[:,1:,:],[[pred_list[i]]],axis=1)
add_dates = [df4.index[-1] + DateOffset(months=x) for x in range(0,13)]
future_dates = pd.DataFrame(index=add_dates[1:],columns=df4.columns)
df_predict = pd.DataFrame(scaler.inverse_transform(pred_list),
                            index=future_dates[-n_input:].index,
columns=['Prediction'])
df_proj = pd.concat([df4,df_predict], axis=1)
df_proj.tail(5)
```

	SalesAmount	Prediction
2020-02-29	NaN	65174.415278
2020-03-31	NaN	61996.016249
2020-04-30	NaN	60737.873723
2020-05-31	NaN	70167.566842
2020-06-30	NaN	55674.230439

```
plot_data = [
    go.Scatter(
        x=df_proj.index,
```

```
    y=df_proj['SalesAmount'],
    name='Actual'
  ),
  go.Scatter(
    x=df_proj.index,
    y=df_proj['Prediction'],
    name='Forecast'
  )
]
plot_layout = go.Layout(
    title='Sales Quantity prediction'
  )
fig = go.Figure(data=plot_data, layout=plot_layout)
#pyoff.iplot(fig)
fig.show(renderer="colab")
```

```
df_predict = pd.DataFrame(scaler.inverse_transform(pred_list),
                              index=future_dates[-n_input:].index,
columns=['Prediction'])
ActFcast = pd.concat([df4,df_predict], axis=1)
ActFcast.tail(10)
```

	SalesAmount	Prediction
2019-02-28	71152.0	NaN
2019-03-31	68024.0	NaN
2019-04-30	59575.0	NaN
2019-05-31	64466.0	NaN
2019-06-30	57192.0	NaN
2019-07-31	73512.0	NaN
2019-08-31	63722.0	NaN
2019-09-30	55871.0	NaN
2019-10-31	72258.0	NaN
2019-11-30	64899.0	NaN
2019-12-31	60565.0	NaN
2020-01-31	74828.0	NaN
2020-02-29	NaN	65174.415278
2020-03-31	NaN	61996.016249
2020-04-30	NaN	60737.873733

General thoughts on sales prediction:

All the algorithms we used tried to find a function(s) for the data`s pattern. It is possible to find patterns from past data and successfully formalize them in real-life sales data. However, in real-life sales data, it is doubtful that these patterns will remain unchanged. Sometimes, ML gets confused by some people with a crystal ball. However, it is crystal clear that ML can only formalize from past data and, therefore, will only make good predictions in the future if future data keeps the underlying pattern (what the model tried to fit best).

2.4 MARKET BASKET ANALYSIS

From predicting sales, we are now moving to analyze our sales transaction IDs (market baskets) to see which items are frequently bought together. This is called **association** rule mining, and we are going to use the **Apriori** algorithm for it. With regard to market basket analysis (products sold within one sales transaction), we want to find frequent patterns, associations, correlations, or causal structures among sets of items. The more customers have bought the same items in one transaction, the more sure we are that products are not combined in coincidence (**Power of Crowds**).

Association rules are typically written like this: {Sales Item1} -> {Sales Item 8}, which means that there is a strong relationship (depending on the user-defined measures of interestingness like support, confidence, or lift, which we will discuss shortly) for customers who have purchased Sales Item1 will also purchase Sales Item8 in the same transaction. In our example, the { Sales Item1} is the **antecedent,** and the { Sales Item 8} is the **consequent.** Both antecedents and consequents can have multiple items. In other words, { Sales Item1, Sales Item 3} -> { Sales Item 8, Sales Item 6} can also be a valid rule.

Support is the relative frequency of the rule within transactions. In many instances, we are looking for high support in order to make sure it is a useful relationship. However, there may be instances where a low support is useful if we are trying to find "**hidden**" relationships.

Confidence is a measure of the reliability of the rule. It denotes the percentage of transactions containing Sales Item 1, which also contains Sales Item 3. It is an estimation of conditioned probability. A confidence level of .5 in the above example would mean that in 50% of the cases where Sales Item 1 and 3 were purchased, the purchase also included Sales Item 8 and Sales Item 6. For product recommendation, a 50% confidence may be perfectly acceptable, but in a regulated environment, this confidence may not be high enough.

Lift is the ratio of the observed support to that expected if the two rules were independent. The basic rule of thumb is that a lift value close to 1 means the rules were completely independent. Lift values > 1 are generally more "interesting" and could indicate a proper rule pattern.

2.4.1 APRIORI

Association rules help us identify the items that occur together frequently in sales transactions (market baskets). Apriori is an algorithm for frequent pattern mining that focuses on generating the most frequent item sets. Apriori generates candidate item sets and has to scan them multiple times to check the support of each item set. That is extremely computationally expensive. That's why we will use the FP Growth algorithm in a second attempt.

```python
import pandas as pd
data = pd.read_excel('/content/gdrive/My Drive/DDDDFolder/DDDD.xlsx')
data.head()
```

	SalesDate	SalesValue	SalesAmount	Customer	SalesTransactionID	SalesItem
0	2018-09-28	8280.0	10	0	0	0
1	2018-09-28	7452.0	10	0	0	0
2	2019-04-23	21114.0	30	0	1	0
3	2019-04-23	7038.0	10	0	1	1

```python
df1 = data[['Customer','SalesTransactionID','SalesItem']]
df1.head()
```

	Customer	SalesTransactionID	SalesItem
0	0	0	0
1	0	0	0
2	0	1	0
3	0	1	1
4	0	1	2

df=df1.groupby ('SalesTransactionID') ['SalesItem']. apply (lambda x: x.reset_index (drop = True)). unstack (). reset_index ()
df.drop('SalesTransactionID',axis=1, inplace=True)
df.head()

	0	1	2	3	4	5	6	7	8	9	10	11	12	13	14	15	16	17	18	19	20	21	22	2:
0	0.0	0.0	NaN	NaN	NaN	NaN	NaN	NaN	NaN	NaN	NaN	NaN	NaN	NaN	NaN	NaN	NaN	NaN	NaN	NaN	NaN	NaN	NaN	NaA
1	0.0	1.0	2.0	NaN	NaN	NaN	NaN	NaN	NaN	NaN	NaN	NaN	NaN	NaN	NaN	NaN	NaN	NaN	NaN	NaN	NaN	NaN	NaN	NaA
2	1.0	1.0	NaN	NaN	NaN	NaN	NaN	NaN	NaN	NaN	NaN	NaN	NaN	NaN	NaN	NaN	NaN	NaN	NaN	NaN	NaN	NaN	NaN	NaA
3	0.0	NaN	NaN	NaN	NaN	NaN	NaN	NaN	NaN	NaN	NaN	NaN	NaN	NaN	NaN	NaN	NaN	NaN	NaN	NaN	NaN	NaN	NaN	NaA
4	0.0	NaN	NaN	NaN	NaN	NaN	NaN	NaN	NaN	NaN	NaN	NaN	NaN	NaN	NaN	NaN	NaN	NaN	NaN	NaN	NaN	NaN	NaN	NaA

5 rows × 446 columns

items = (df[0].unique())
items

array([0.000e+00, 1.000e+00, 2.000e+00, ..., 9.060e+02, 1.536e+03,
       3.750e+03])

encoded_vals = []
def custom():
  for index, row in df.iterrows():
    labels = {}
    uncommons = list(set(items) - set(row))

```
      commons = list(set(items).intersection(row))
      for uc in uncommons:
        labels[uc] = 0
      for com in commons:
        labels[com] = 1
      encoded_vals.append(labels)
custom()
ohe_df = pd.DataFrame(encoded_vals)
print(ohe_df)
```

```
           1.0      2.0      3.0      4.0      ...  3742.0  3745.0  3750.0  0.0
0            0        0        0        0      ...      0       0       0      1
1            1        1        0        0      ...      0       0       0      1
2            1        0        0        0      ...      0       0       0      0
3            0        0        0        0      ...      0       0       0      1
4            0        0        0        0      ...      0       0       0      1
...        ...      ...      ...      ...      ...    ...     ...     ...    ...
48421        0        0        0        0      ...      0       0       0      0
48422        0        0        0        0      ...      0       0       0      0
48423        0        0        0        0      ...      0       0       0      0
48424        0        0        0        0      ...      0       0       0      0
48425        0        0        0        0      ...      0       0       0      0

[48426 rows x 1549 columns]
```

```
from mlxtend.frequent_patterns import apriori
from mlxtend.frequent_patterns import association_rules
freq_items      =      apriori(ohe_df,      min_support=0.006,
use_colnames=True
freq_items
```

	support	itemsets
0	0.006732	(6.0)
1	0.021270	(7.0)
2	0.024326	(8.0)
3	0.021600	(9.0)
4	0.018812	(13.0)
...	...	...
1044	0.006174	(312.0, 98.0, 104.0, 103.0)
1045	0.007228	(312.0, 98.0, 108.0, 103.0)
1046	0.006422	(312.0, 108.0, 98.0, 104.0)
1047	0.006463	(104.0, 108.0, 110.0, 103.0)
1048	0.006257	(312.0, 108.0, 104.0, 103.0)

1049 rows × 2 columns

freq_items.to_excel('Export&Supportvalues.xlsx')

rules = association_rules(freq_items, metric="confidence", min_threshold=0.006)
rules

	antecedents	consequents	antecedent support	consequent support	support	confidence	lift	leverage	conviction
0	(8.0)	(7.0)	0.024326	0.021270	0.008095	0.332767	15.645237	0.007577	1.466850
1	(7.0)	(8.0)	0.021270	0.024326	0.008095	0.380583	15.645237	0.007577	1.575148
2	(20.0)	(7.0)	0.058584	0.021270	0.007062	0.120550	5.667717	0.005816	1.112889
3	(7.0)	(20.0)	0.021270	0.058584	0.007062	0.332039	5.667717	0.005816	1.409387
4	(83.0)	(7.0)	0.040784	0.021270	0.006422	0.157468	7.403459	0.005555	1.161654
...									
2569	(104.0, 103.0)	(312.0, 108.0)	0.018275	0.012597	0.006257	0.342373	27.179917	0.006027	1.501464
2570	(312.0)	(104.0, 108.0, 103.0)	0.021951	0.010346	0.006257	0.285042	27.551816	0.006030	1.384214
2571	(108.0)	(312.0, 104.0, 103.0)	0.034176	0.007124	0.006257	0.183082	25.698285	0.006013	1.215392
2572	(104.0)	(312.0, 108.0, 103.0)	0.049911	0.009107	0.006257	0.125362	13.765944	0.005802	1.132918
2573	(103.0)	(312.0, 108.0, 104.0)	0.043840	0.007455	0.006257	0.142723	19.145382	0.005930	1.157788

2574 rows × 9 columns

import matplotlib.pyplot as plt
plt.scatter(rules['support'], rules['confidence'], alpha=0.2,color='brown')
plt.xlabel('support')

227

```
plt.ylabel('confidence')
plt.title('Support vs Confidence')
plt.show()
```

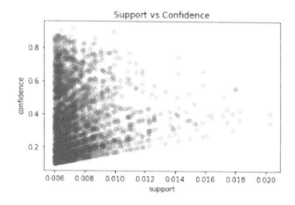

```
plt.scatter(rules['support'], rules['lift'], alpha=0.2,color='orange')
plt.xlabel('support')
plt.ylabel('lift')
plt.title('Support vs Lift')
plt.show()
```

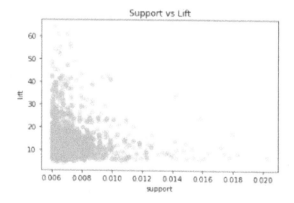

A Network Graph is one way to display the Apriori Market Basket visual results. The radius of the nodes could be the measured lift, while the edges' (the link between the nodes) thickness could show confidence. The different product (or customer) segments could be color-coordinated.

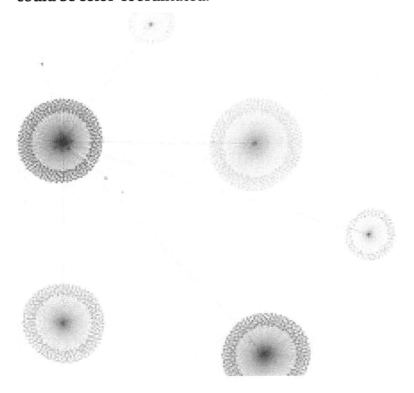

2.4.2 FPGROWTH

Now, we will use a similar approach to Apriori, but this time using Frequent Pattern Growth (FPGrowth) with Spark.

```
%%capture
!sudo apt-get update --fix-missing
!apt-get install openjdk-8-jdk-headless -qq > /dev/null
!wget -q https://archive.apache.org/dist/spark/spark-3.0.0/spark-3.0.0-bin-hadoop3.2.tgz
#!wget -q https://downloads.apache.org/spark/spark-3.0.0/spark-3.0.0-bin-hadoop3.2.tgz
!mv spark-3.0.0-bin-hadoop3.2.tgz sparkkk
!tar xf sparkkk
!pip install -q findspark

import os
os.environ["JAVA_HOME"] = "/usr/lib/jvm/java-8-openjdk-amd64"
os.environ["SPARK_HOME"] = "/content/spark-3.0.0-bin-hadoop3.2"
import findspark
findspark.init()
from pyspark.sql import SparkSession
spark = SparkSession.builder.master("local[*]").getOrCreate()
from pyspark.sql import SparkSession
spark = SparkSession \
  .builder \
  .appName('fpgrowth') \
  .getOrCreate()
spark
```

```
SparkSession - in-memory
SparkContext
Spark UI

Version
    v3.0.0
Master
    local[*]
AppName
    pyspark-shell
```

```python
from google.colab import files
from pyspark.sql import functions as F
from pyspark.ml.fpm import FPGrowth
import pandas
sparkdata = spark.createDataFrame(data)
basketdata = sparkdata.dropDuplicates(['SalesTransactionID',
'SalesItem']).sort('SalesTransactionID')
basketdata =
basketdata.groupBy("SalesTransactionID").agg(F.collect_list("SalesI
tem")).sort('SalesTransactionID')
```

```python
#Frequent Pattern Growth – FP Growth is a method of mining
frequent itemsets
fpGrowth = FPGrowth(itemsCol="collect_list(SalesItem)",
minSupport=0.006, minConfidence=0.006)
model = fpGrowth.fit(basketdata)
# Display frequent itemsets.
model.freqItemsets.show()
items = model.freqItemsets
# Display generated association rules.
model.associationRules.show()
rules = model.associationRules
# transform examines the input items against all the association
rules and summarize the
# consequents as prediction
model.transform(basketdata).show()
transformed = model.transform(basketdata)
```

```
+--------------------+----+
|              items|freq|
+--------------------+----+
|             [257]| 432|
|              [20]|2837|
|             [104]|2417|
|         [104, 20]| 981|
|            [1491]| 432|
|             [110]|2172|
|        [110, 104]| 745|
|    [110, 104, 20]| 476|
|         [110, 20]| 765|
|            [1495]| 431|
|             [103]|2123|
|        [103, 110]| 671|
|   [103, 110, 104]| 445|
|[103, 110, 104, 20]| 348|
|    [103, 110, 20]| 444|
|        [103, 104]| 885|
|    [103, 104, 20]| 572|
|         [103, 20]| 861|
|             [179]| 431|
|              [67]|1975|
+--------------------+----+
only showing top 20 rows
```

```
+------------+----------+--------------------+------------------+
| antecedent|consequent|          confidence|              lift|
+------------+----------+--------------------+------------------+
|       [128]|      [67]| 0.3379978471474704|  8.28753607390552|
|       [128]|      [91]|0.34230355220667386|10.666918802548512|
|       [128]|     [104]|  0.38751345532831| 7.764057338737584|
|       [128]|      [92]|0.3153928955866523| 9.648273128034885|
|       [128]|     [103]|0.35522066738428415| 8.102645331489093|
|[91, 92, 67]|     [104]| 0.7577197149643705| 15.18135495112313|
|[91, 92, 67]|     [103]| 0.7197149643705463|16.416823770423022|
|   [83, 103]|      [67]| 0.519327731092437|12.733653015636635|
|   [83, 103]|     [110]|0.5210084033613446|11.616184595385116|
|   [83, 103]|     [104]|0.5495798319327732|11.011151403051912|
|   [83, 103]|      [20]|0.6201680672268908|10.585921333637438|
|   [83, 103]|     [120]|0.5277310924369748| 14.42206878236622|
|   [83, 103]|     [108]|0.5478991596638656|16.031761151590544|
|       [316]|     [514]|0.3029087261785356|10.440325960086666|
|       [316]|      [83]|0.35907723169508526| 8.804391909906936|
|       [316]|      [67]|0.30090270812437314| 7.377982047408047|
|       [316]|     [104]|0.3350050150451354| 6.7120202145534655|
|       [316]|     [103]|0.32898696088264795| 7.504249914132412|
|       [316]|      [63]|0.5536609829488466| 20.250443172417555|
|       [316]|      [64]| 0.506519558676028|21.109050041691336|
+------------+----------+--------------------+------------------+
only showing top 20 rows
```

```
+-----------------+------------------------+---------------------+
|SalesTransactionID|collect_list(SalesItem)|           prediction|
+-----------------+------------------------+---------------------+
|                0|                    [0]|                  []|
|                1|              [0, 1, 2]|                  []|
|                2|                    [1]|                  []|
|                3|                    [0]|                  []|
|                4|                    [0]|                  []|
|                5|                    [0]|                  []|
|                6|                    [2]|                  []|
|                7|                    [2]|                  []|
|                8|                    [0]|                  []|
|               10|                 [1, 0]|                  []|
|               11|                    [0]|                  []|
|               12|                 [4, 3]|                  []|
|               13|                    [5]|                  []|
|               15|              [7, 8, 9]|[83, 20, 108, 514...|
|               16|      [17, 15, 16, 20, ...|[101, 104, 110, 1...|
|               17|                   [21]|                  []|
|               18|                   [22]|                  []|
|               19|      [33, 41, 27, 34, ...|                  []|
|               20|      [59, 50, 57, 60, ...|                  []|
|               21|                   [62]|                  []|
+-----------------+------------------------+---------------------+
only showing top 20 rows
```

# Convert the Spark DataFrame back to a Pandas DataFrame using Arrow
result_pdf = items.select("*").toPandas()
result_pdf.head()

result_pdf.to_excel('result_pdfItemsFreq.xlsx')

rules_pdf = rules.select("*").toPandas()
rules_pdf.head()

rules_pdf.to_excel('rules_pdfAnteConseConfLift.xlsx')

transformed_pdf = transformed.select("*").toPandas()
transformed_pdf.head()

transformed_pdf.to_excel('transformed_pdfSalesTransactionIDCol lectListPred.xlsx')

Did you just notice the column "Predicted" in the

file "transformed_pdfSalesTransactionIDCollectListPred"? This means that if you bought items 7, 8, and 9, you should also be highly interested in items 83, 20, 108, 514, 110, and so on. This is already a recommendation and will lead us to the next chapter.

2.5 RECOMMENDER

Simple is better than complex (Zen of Python)

To recap our last chapter about the Apriori algorithm, we learned that products are often related to each other. For example, if one customer buys product A, that customer will most likely also purchase product B because you cannot run product A without product B, or it just makes sense to buy both of them together for other reasons. Therefore, customers purchase more than one product within one sales transaction ID **(associated)**.

If we ask Alexa, "What's the difference between **"association"** and "**recommendation?**", Amazon's voice assistant should tell us something like (okay, it seems that also Amazon still has some way to go with its AI, at least by the 07.02.2021 Alexa was not able to tell me the difference about it):

"If we check our sales transaction ID (market basket) for frequently bought together products, that is called an associative analysis. While "customers who bought this item also bought that item" is a recommendation analysis."

See an example taken from my Amazon account:

Or take Google's Youtube: thanks for sharing Google, no one knows me like you do!

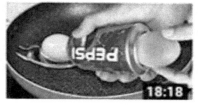

40 GROßARTIGE KÜCHEN-TRICKS, VON DENEN DU NICH...

5-MINUTEN-TRICKS

Recommended for you

Recommending customers the things they might be most interested in is what we are going to do now, building an ML recommending application. We will move one step out of the market basket (on the sales transaction ID level) into the overall buying behavior (which items our customers bought) of our customers. We aim to recommend a specific product because many other similar customers have also purchased this article. We do not have any labeled data available that tells us which customers are similar to each other. Still, we will extract similarities between customers simply from their connection to the same items they bought in the past. We anticipate that the similar preferences customers had in the past will also extend to the future. So, "if customer A purchases products 2,5 and 6 (not necessarily within the same basket) and customer B purchases products 2, 5, 6, and 9, then we can estimate that customer A is also interested in product 9 (recommended)". If customer A is similar to customer B, and customer B purchased item C, then the system can recommend item C to customer A, even if customer A has not yet purchased any items similar to item C. The kind of ML algorithms that build on this concept are called collaborative filtering (CF) algorithms. CF is an ML algorithm that collects preferences or taste information from many customers (collaborative, since it combines collected information) and uses this information to make automatic predictions (filtering out less probable options to find the most probable prediction) about the interests of other customers. CF is one of the most widely researched and implemented recommendation algorithms (according to Christopher R. Aberger, Recommender: An Analysis of **Collaborative Filtering** Techniques).

This collaborative filtering approach focuses on finding customers who have purchased nearly the same quantity of specific products **(implicit).** Now, we can look at the products these similar customers have bought and link those products back to the items we want to recommend to the customer. Of course, we will only recommend items that the customer has not yet purchased and only recommend the items with the highest amount purchased. Suppose we can simply rely on similar customers' tastes and preference histories. In that case, the role of a collaborative model is to match customers who share the same preferences so they can be mutually offered recommendations.

Explicit is better than Implicit (Zen of Python)

..but implicit is better than nothing. The question is whether the customer ever bought a specific item and if you want to consider the amount as well: implicitly, did a customer ever buy a particular item, yes or no (vs. if yes, how many)? If a customer would rate our products, that would be **explicit** feedback. Explicit feedback is critical nowadays due to the vast offerings our globalized online shopping has made possible, but it is not covered in our book. We will recommend the sales quantity customers buy on a binary level (purchased yes or no) because I believe this is most relevant to most readers. I think that in real life, we often only have implicit feedback at our fingertips.

Let us clarify why we want to recommend articles to our customers. With regards to the possible benefits of recommending engines depending on our sales data and company, there seem to be two poles to this:

1. E Commerce Shop:

Imagine working for a considerable e-commerce platform that sells nearly all the products we can imagine. A CF approach is very fruitful for such a platform since we have a straightforward connection between our service and our end customer. Chances are very high that we will be able to increase our overall sales via usefully recommending articles to our customers so that the customer will hopefully shop more than without any recommendation stimulus.

2. Supporting our Salesforce colleagues

In many industries, interacting with the customers and knowing what the customer should be interested in is not easy. Just think of the legal boundaries and existing compliance rules and regulations in your company if we are working in a medical business, financial service sector, etc. So it will not be as easy and meaningful to predict what articles our customers should be highly interested in. This is because we cannot quickly tell who other similar customers are (and therefore, we can not always give a satisfying recommendation) as long as we only count on the customer`s sales history. Imagine we have one customer who is selling medical devices. By analyzing this customer`s sales history, we found other similar customers. But of course, the other customers (let's say they are all hospitals) offer very different procedures, so it might end up that even though they have all purchased one specific item, the similar customer has not yet. But after recommending this item to that customer, the customer will tell us that "there is no sense in recommending me this item since we do not at all provide the specific procedure for this item". So, is there no use in using CF in this case? Yes, there is. Even in this highly regulated area, the recommendation still has its benefits because it can still be a very supportive analysis for our salesforce colleagues to prepare before their customer interaction. We aim to support our salesforce in preparing before their "customer service action". If possible, we want to ensure that our customers buy all the devices they need from us. We want to be at least aware that a specific customer should have purchased our product but hasn't yet. Maybe the customer just needs more salesforce penetration for that product, or our competitor has already made the deal. The worst thing would be if we did not know at all that our customer is also interested in a specific product. We try to ensure we are aware of that by predicting what the customer most likely should be interested in (as a service for our sales colleagues).

Using apriori during our market basket analysis, we learned which items were frequently bought together in one transaction. This knowledge is essential for, e.g., discount and marketing activities and settings. With CF, we are moving even one step closer to our customer, giving him product recommendations on an individual level without any extra effort from the customer's side (since we are just looking at his past sales data as implicit feedback and recommend products to him he has not yet purchased but should be highly interested in, because other similar customers did buy this item very often). Let us now use this wisdom of crowds (fancier expression than

CF) and full-throttle our collaborative filtering recommendation engine.

2.5.1 COLLABORATIVE FILTERING

Complex is better than complicated (Zen of Python).

Implicit feedback, like the number of items purchased, clicks on a website, movies watched, etc., is not explicit feedback. So it could be that even if we bought a specific book, we do not like it while reading it. Even though this is a disadvantage of implicit feedback, we often do not have explicit customer feedback in real life, so we have to stick to implicit feedback. Or suppose the amount of implicit feedback outweighs the amount of explicit feedback. In that case, we might decide to build our recommending engine on implicit data (sometimes, a mass of data rules over less data, even with better quality). We look for **associations** between customers, not between products. Therefore, collaborative filtering relies only on observed customer behavior to make recommendations —with no information about the customers or the items required.

Our technique will be based on the following observations:

- Customers who purchased products in a similar quantity share one or more hidden preferences (latent or hidden features).
- Customers with shared preferences will likely purchase products in a similar way.

There are primarily two ways to find the group of k similar customers:

- **Memory based**: This neighborhood-based approach calculates the similarity between two customers or items and then produces a prediction for the customer by taking the (weighted) average of all ratings. Cosine similarity is often used to find the nearest neighbors and calculate the ratings for the items not rated by the specific customer to whom we want to recommend items. This algorithm is commonly called K-nearest neighbor (KNN). Neighbor, in this case, means looking for customers who have bought similar items.

- **Model based**: It uses the notion of **matrix factorization** (modern ML algorithms like SVD or deep learning models like Restricted Boltzmann machines) to discover patterns in the training data and predict the customer's ratings. We factorize a customer-interactions matrix into customer factors and item factors. We multiply by item factors with a given customer to get predicted "ratings" for all items. Finally, we can return the top k-rated items for this customer. Model-based approaches uncover **latent** factors that can be used to construct training data ratings and handle **sparsity** better than memory-based techniques.

Trying to conduct collaborative filtering, we could have a look at Yifan Hu, Yehuda Koren, and Chris Volinskys`paper:

http://yifanhu.net/PUB/cf.pdf.

Meta and Spotify are supposed to use the approach mentioned in this paper. Have you read it? Did you understand it and know how to put this into Python code? Frankly, I can say yes to question 1, but definitely no to question 2. In case you're answering similarly, feel welcome to join me through all this step by step for the sake of better understanding.

We will divide our recommending task into two main steps:

- Calculate the similarity between customers (customer-customer matrix) and articles (item-item matrix)
- Implement the recommender model.

2.5.2 MEASURING SIMILARITY

How do we measure similarity?

How can we tell how similar one customer is compared to another customer?

Or how similar one item is to other items?

To answer this question, it is helpful to state that the similarity approach complements distance. While the distance between two points can be obtained using the Euclidean distance - calculating the length of a straight line connecting two points- similarity is about "how close" the points are. The similarity value is usually expressed as a number between 0 and 1, where 0 is a low similarity, and 1 is a high similarity.

Let's break this down into simple Google Sheets/ Microsoft Excel formula (below sheet screenshots used Google Sheets, which you can also find in my Github repository: https://github.com/ DAR-DatenanalyseRehberg):

Imagine 9 Customers have purchased these 7 Sales items as follows (1 means purchased, 0 means not purchased), then the "PurchaseHistory" Tab looks like this:

	A	B	C	D	E	F	G	H
1	Customer	Sales Item 1	Sales Item 2	Sales Item 3	Sales Item 4	Sales Item 5	Sales Item 6	Sales Item 7
2	Customer 1	0	0	1	0	0	0	0
3	Customer 2	0	0	0	1	0	0	0
4	Customer 3	0	1	0	0	0	0	0
5	Customer 4	1	0	0	0	0	0	0
6	Customer 5	0	0	0	1	0	0	0
7	Customer 6	0	1	0	0	0	0	1
8	Customer 7	0	1	0	0	0	0	0
9	Customer 8	0	0	1	0	0	0	0
10	Customer 9	1	0	1	1	1	1	1

The normalized data will look like this in tab "PurchHistNorm":

	A	B	C	D	E	F	G	H	KA
1	Customer	Sales Item 1	Sales Item 2	Sales Item 3	Sales Item 4	Sales Item 5	Sales Item 6	Sales Item 7	Magnitude
2	Customer 1	0.000	0.000	1.000	0.000	0.000	0.000	0.000	1.000
3	Customer 2	0.000	0.000	0.000	1.000	0.000	0.000	0.000	1.000
4	Customer 3	0.000	1.000	0.000	0.000	0.000	0.000	0.000	1.000
5	Customer 4	1.000	0.000	0.000	0.000	0.000	0.000	0.000	1.000
6	Customer 5	0.000	0.000	0.000	1.000	0.000	0.000	0.000	1.000
7	Customer 6	0.000	0.707	0.000	0.000	0.000	0.000	0.707	1.414
8	Customer 7	0.000	1.000	0.000	0.000	0.000	0.000	0.000	1.000
9	Customer 8	0.000	0.000	1.000	0.000	0.000	0.000	0.000	1.000
10	Customer 9	0.408	0.000	0.408	0.408	0.408	0.408	0.408	2.449
535	L2	1.08012345	1.58113883	1.471960144	1.471960144	0.4082482905	0.4082482905	0.8164965809	

Because for eg. customer 1 the magnitude is:

	A	B	C	D	E	F	G	H	KA
									=PurchHist!D2/$KA2
1	Customer	Sales Item 1	Sales Item 2	Sales Item 3	Sales Item 4	Sales Item 5	Sales Item 6	Sales Item 7	Magnitude
2	Customer 1	0.000	0.000	1.000	0.000	0.000	0.000	0.000	1.000
3	Customer 2	0.000	0.000	0.000	1.000	0.000	0.000	0.000	1.000
4	Customer 3	0.000	1.000	0.000	0.000	0.000	0.000	0.000	1.000
5	Customer 4	1.000	0.000	0.000	0.000	0.000	0.000	0.000	1.000
6	Customer 5	0.000	0.000	0.000	1.000	0.000	0.000	0.000	1.000
7	Customer 6	0.000	0.707	0.000	0.000	0.000	0.000	0.707	1.414
8	Customer 7	0.000	1.000	0.000	0.000	0.000	0.000	0.000	1.000
9	Customer 8	0.000	0.000	1.000	0.000	0.000	0.000	0.000	1.000
10	Customer 9	0.408	0.000	0.408	0.408	0.408	0.408	0.408	2.449
535	L2	1.08012345	1.58113883	1.471960144	1.471960144	0.4082482905	0.4082482905	0.8164965809	

=SQRT(SUMSQ(PurchHist!B2:H2))

	A	B	C	D	E	F	G	H	KA
1	Customer	Sales Item 1	Sales Item 2	Sales Item 3	Sales Item 4	Sales Item 5	Sales Item 6	Sales Item 7	**Magnitude**
2	Customer 1	0.000	0.000	1.000	0.000	0.000	0.000	0.000	1.000
3	Customer 2	0.000	0.000	0.000	1.000	0.000	0.000	0.000	1.000
4	Customer 3	0.000	1.000	0.000	0.000	0.000	0.000	0.000	1.000
5	Customer 4	1.000	0.000	0.000	0.000	0.000	0.000	0.000	1.000
6	Customer 5	0.000	0.000	0.000	1.000	0.000	0.000	0.000	1.000
7	Customer 6	0.000	0.707	0.000	0.000	0.000	0.000	0.707	1.414
8	Customer 7	0.000	1.000	0.000	0.000	0.000	0.000	0.000	1.000
9	Customer 8	0.000	0.000	1.000	0.000	0.000	0.000	0.000	1.000
10	Customer 9	0.408	0.000	0.408	0.408	0.408	0.408	0.408	2.449
535	L2	1.08012345	1.58113883	1.471960144	1.471960144	0.4082482905	0.4082482905	0.8164965809	

=SQRT(SUMSQ(B57:E$10))

	A	B	C	D	E	F	G	H	KA
1	Customer	Sales Item 1	Sales Item 2	Sales Item 3	Sales Item 4	Sales Item 5	Sales Item 6	Sales Item 7	**Magnitude**
2	Customer 1	0.000	0.000	1.000	0.000	0.000	0.000	0.000	1.000
3	Customer 2	0.000	0.000	0.000	1.000	0.000	0.000	0.000	1.000
4	Customer 3	0.000	1.000	0.000	0.000	0.000	0.000	0.000	1.000
5	Customer 4	1.000	0.000	0.000	0.000	0.000	0.000	0.000	1.000
6	Customer 5	0.000	0.000	0.000	1.000	0.000	0.000	0.000	1.000
7	Customer 6	0.000	0.707	0.000	0.000	0.000	0.000	0.707	1.414
8	Customer 7	0.000	1.000	0.000	0.000	0.000	0.000	0.000	1.000
9	Customer 8	0.000	0.000	1.000	0.000	0.000	0.000	0.000	1.000
10	Customer 9	0.408	0.000	0.408	0.408	0.408	0.408	0.408	2.449
535	L2	1.08012345	1.58113883	1.471960144	1.471960144	0.4082482905	0.4082482905	0.8164965809	

So finally, the item-item similarity matrix looks like this:

f_x	=SUMPRODUCT(PurchHistNorm!B2:B10,PurchHistNorm!B2:B10)/(PurchHistNorm!B535*PurchHistNorm!B535)							
	A	B	C	D	E	F	G	H
1		Sales Item 1	Sales Item 2	Sales Item 3	Sales Item 4	Sales Item 5	Sales Item 6	Sales Item 7
2	Sales Item 1	1						
3	Sales Item 2	0	1					
4	Sales Item 3	0.10482848	0	1				
5	Sales Item 4	0.10482848	0	0.0769230	1			
6	Sales Item 5	0.37796447	0	0.2773500	0.2773500	1		
7	Sales Item 6	0.37796447	0	0.2773500	0.2773500	1	1	
8	Sales Item 7	0.1889822	0.38729833	0.1386750	0.1386750	0.5	0.5	1

Certainly a product is always highest correlated with itself (Sales Item 1 with Sales Item 1 correlates perfectly scoring a 1).

Which similarity measure to use?

If the data is subject to **grade inflation** (different customers may be using different scales), use Pearson. If our data is dense (almost all attributes have non-zero values) and the magnitude of the attribute values is important, use distance measures such as Euclidean or Manhattan. For our sparse univariate data example, we will stick to Cosine Similarity.

2.5.3 BASIC COLLABORATIVE FILTERING

Sparse is better than dense (Zen of Python).

Our baseline data, on which we will build our recommending engine, has this shape: 36 unique customers (from 0 to 35) and 3751 items. Did they buy 3751 different items? Let's check our data once more, focusing on SalesAmount. We see that some customers purchased some items with a sales amount of 0 (0 quantity, in other words). Since these transactions do not make sense for our recommending model, we will delete these rows beforehand (Data Cleansing).

```
import pandas as pd
data = pd.read_excel('/content/gdrive/My Drive/DDDDFolder/DDDD.xlsx')
data.head()
```

	SalesDate	SalesValue	SalesAmount	Customer	SalesTransactionID	SalesItem
0	2018-09-28	8280.0	10	0	0	0
1	2018-09-28	7452.0	10	0	0	0
2	2019-04-23	21114.0	30	0	1	0
3	2019-04-23	7038.0	10	0	1	1

Check for Sparsity:

DataPrep = data[['SalesItem', 'SalesAmount', 'Customer']] #we will only use SalesItem, SalesAmount and Customer for our recommending purpose
DataPrep.head()

	SalesItem	SalesAmount	Customer
0	0	10	0
1	0	10	0
2	0	30	0
3	1	10	0

```
DataPrep.info()

<class 'pandas.core.frame.DataFrame'>
RangeIndex: 341422 entries, 0 to 341421
Data columns (total 3 columns):
 #   Column       Non-Null Count    Dtype
---  ------       --------------    -----
 0   SalesItem    341422 non-null   int64
 1   SalesAmount  341422 non-null   int64
 2   Customer     341422 non-null   int64
dtypes: int64(3)
memory usage: 7.8 MB
```

DataGrouped = DataPrep.groupby(['Customer', 'SalesItem']).sum().reset_index() # Group together
DataGrouped.head()

	Customer	SalesItem	SalesAmount
0	0	0	281
1	0	1	158
2	0	2	13
3	0	768	1

import numpy as np
customers = list(np.sort(DataGrouped.Customer.unique())) # why 36 unique customers in a list and not 35?
products = list(DataGrouped.SalesItem.unique()) # Get our unique 3725 unique products that were purchased

```
quantity = list(DataGrouped.SalesAmount) # All of our purchases
#list function is a list of values. So customers now stores 36 unique
customers. See example for customers: customers
```

```
from pandas import DataFrame
DfCustomerUnique = DataFrame(customers,columns=['Customer'])
DfCustomerUnique.head()
```

	Customer
0	0
1	1
2	2
3	3

```
from scipy import sparse
from pandas.api.types import CategoricalDtype
rows                                                         =
DataGrouped.Customer.astype(CategoricalDtype(categories=custo
mers)).cat.codes # We have got 35 unique customers, which make
up 13837 data rows (index)
# Get the associated row indices
cols = DataGrouped.SalesItem.astype(CategoricalDtype(categories=
products)).cat.codes # We have got unique 3725 SalesItems, making
up 13837 data rows (index)
# Get the associated column indices
#Compressed Sparse Row matrix
PurchaseSparse    =    sparse.csr_matrix((quantity,    (rows,    cols)),
shape=(len(customers), len(products))) #len of customers=35, len
of products=3725
#csr_matrix((data, (row_ind, col_ind)), [shape=(M, N)])
```

#where data, row_ind and col_ind satisfy the relationship a[row_ind[k], col_ind[k]] = data[k]. , see https://docs.scipy.org/doc/scipy/reference/generated/scipy.sparse.csr_matrix.html

PurchaseSparse

#a sparse matrix is not a pandas dataframe, but sparse matrices are efficient for row slicing and fast matrix vector products

```
<35x3725 sparse matrix of type '<class 'numpy.longlong'>'
        with 13837 stored elements in Compressed Sparse Row format>
```

#We have 35 customers with 3725 items. For these user/item interactions, 13837 of these items had a purchase.

#In terms of sparsity of the matrix, that makes:

MatrixSize = PurchaseSparse.shape[0]*PurchaseSparse.shape[1] # 130375 possible interactions in the matrix (35 unique customers * 3725 unique SalesItems=130375)

PurchaseAmount = len(PurchaseSparse.nonzero()[0]) # 13837 SalesItems interacted with;

sparsity = 100*(1 - (PurchaseAmount/MatrixSize))

sparsity

Since we will use Matrix Factorization for our collaborative filtering, it should not be a problem that 89.3% of the interaction matrix is sparse. In plain English, 89,3% means that only 10,7% of our customer-item interactions are already filled, meaning that customers have not purchased most items. It is said that collaborative filtering can even work well with even more sparse data. We can prove that it works when checking our decent recommendations. Cosine Similarity is a good measure for sparse data, so we will stick to Cosine (instead of Pearson, Euclidean, or Manhattan).

We have already discussed sparsity. However, we will start with a simple recommender before we move on to more advanced techniques that also use optimization for sparse matrices.

#for every dataset we will add a 1 as purchased. That means, that this customer has purchased this item, no matter how many. We use this binary data for our recommending. Another approach would be to use the SalesAmount and

#normalize it, in case you want to treat the Amount of SalesItems

purchased as a kind of taste factor, meaning that someone who bought SalesItem x 100 times, while another Customer bought that same SalesItem x only 5 times does
#not like it as much. Normalizing means to standardize continuous features by subtracting the mean and dividing by the standard deviation, so that features with large scale will not dominate. I believe, that very often in Sales a binary approach makes more sense, but of course that depends on the data.

```
def create_DataBinary(DataGrouped):
  DataBinary = DataPrep.copy()
  DataBinary['PurchasedYes'] = 1
  return DataBinary
DataBinary = create_DataBinary(DataGrouped)
DataBinary.head()
```

	SalesItem	SalesAmount	Customer	PurchasedYes
0	0	10	0	1
1	0	10	0	1
2	0	30	0	1
3	1	10	0	1

```
data2=DataBinary.drop(['SalesAmount'], axis=1)
data2.head()
```

	SalesItem	Customer	PurchasedYes
0	0	0	1
1	0	0	1
2	0	0	1

#for better convenience we add I for Item for every SalesItem. Otherwise we would only have customer and SalesItem Numbers, which can be a little bit puzzling.

```
data2['SalesItem'] = 'I' + data2['SalesItem'].astype(str)

DfMatrix     =     pd.pivot_table(data2,     values='PurchasedYes',
index='Customer', columns='SalesItem')
```

DfMatrix.head()

SalesItem	I0	I1	I10	I100	I1000	I1001	I1002	I1003	I1004	I1005	I1006	I1007	I1008	I1009	I101	I1010	I1011
Customer																	
0	1.0	1.0	NaN	NaN	NaN	NaN	NaN	NaN	NaN	NaN	NaN	NaN	NaN	NaN	NaN	NaN	NaN
1	NaN	NaN	NaN	NaN	NaN	NaN	NaN	NaN	NaN	NaN	NaN	NaN	NaN	NaN	NaN	NaN	NaN
2	NaN	NaN	1.0	1.0	1.0	NaN	NaN	NaN	NaN	1.0	1.0	NaN	NaN	NaN	1.0	NaN	NaN
3	NaN	NaN	1.0	NaN	NaN	NaN	NaN	NaN	NaN	NaN	NaN	NaN	NaN	NaN	1.0	NaN	NaN
4	NaN	NaN	NaN	1.0	NaN	NaN	NaN	NaN	NaN	NaN	1.0	NaN	NaN	NaN	1.0	NaN	NaN

5 rows × 3725 columns

#Since we are only using 1 and 0, we do not need to think about normalization, which is one method of **scaling**. Normalization reduces the scale of the data to be in a range from 0 to 1:
Xnormalized = X-Xmin / (Xmax-Xmin)
Another form of scaling is standardization, which reduces the scale of the data to have a mean(μ) of 0 and a standard deviation(σ) of 1:
Xstandardized = X-μ / σ
But talk is cheap, let`s check to see that even if we would normalize, the result is the same, of course:

DfMatrix=DfMatrix.fillna(0) #NaN values need to get replaced by 0, meaning they have not been purchased yet.
DfMatrixNorm3 = (DfMatrix-DfMatrix.min())/(DfMatrix.max()-DfMatrix.min())
DfMatrixNorm3.head()
#the proof is in the pudding. But we will come back to normalization later on again, when we will take real Sales Amount into consideration for recommending as well.

SalesItem	I0	I1	I10	I100	I1000	I1001	I1002	I1003	I1004	I1005	I1006	I1007	I1008	I1009	I101	I1010	I1011	I1012	I1013	I1014	I1015	I101
Customer																						
0	1.0	1.0	0.0	0.0	0.0	0.0	0.0	0.0	0.0	0.0	0.0	0.0	0.0	0.0	0.0	0.0	0.0	0.0	0.0	0.0	0.0	0
1	0.0	0.0	0.0	0.0	0.0	0.0	0.0	0.0	0.0	0.0	0.0	0.0	0.0	0.0	0.0	0.0	0.0	0.0	0.0	0.0	0.0	0
2	0.0	0.0	1.0	1.0	1.0	0.0	0.0	0.0	0.0	1.0	1.0	0.0	0.0	0.0	1.0	0.0	0.0	0.0	0.0	1.0	0.0	0
3	0.0	0.0	1.0	0.0	0.0	0.0	0.0	0.0	0.0	0.0	0.0	0.0	0.0	0.0	1.0	0.0	0.0	0.0	0.0	0.0	0.0	0
4	0.0	0.0	0.0	1.0	0.0	0.0	0.0	0.0	0.0	0.0	1.0	0.0	0.0	0.0	1.0	0.0	0.0	0.0	0.0	0.0	0.0	0

5 rows × 3725 columns

#we need to bring our pivot table into the desired format, via reset_index and rename_axis.

DfResetted = DfMatrix.reset_index().rename_axis(None, axis=1)
DfResetted.head()

#Now each row represents one customer`s buying behaviour: 1 means the customer has purchased, NaN the customer has not yet purchased it

Customer	I0	I1	I10	I100	I1000	I1001	I1002	I1003	I1004	I1005	I1006	I1007	I1008	I1009	I101	I1010	I101
0	0	1.0	1.0	0.0	0.0	0.0	0.0	0.0	0.0	0.0	0.0	0.0	0.0	0.0	0.0	0.0	0.0	0
1	1	0.0	0.0	0.0	0.0	0.0	0.0	0.0	0.0	0.0	0.0	0.0	0.0	0.0	0.0	0.0	0.0	0
2	2	0.0	0.0	1.0	1.0	1.0	0.0	0.0	0.0	0.0	1.0	1.0	0.0	0.0	0.0	1.0	0.0	0
3	3	0.0	0.0	1.0	0.0	0.0	0.0	0.0	0.0	0.0	0.0	0.0	0.0	0.0	0.0	1.0	0.0	0
4	4	0.0	0.0	0.0	1.0	0.0	0.0	0.0	0.0	0.0	1.0	0.0	0.0	0.0	1.0	0.0	0

5 rows × 3726 columns

DfMatrix.shape

(35, 3725)

df=DfResetted #now working: because Customer must be nvarchar! If customer is int, then failure during CustItemSimilarity!

#we need to replace the NaN values with a 0, because our function will not work on NaN values.
#Please note, that we are only checking if a specific customer bought a specific item, yes or no. That is called binary. If customer bought a specific item, that means 1. If not, then 0. Because of this binary problem there is
#no use in using any further scaling techniques.

df=df.fillna(0)
df.head()

Customer	I0	I1	I10	I100	I1000	I1001	I1002	I1003	I1004	I1005	I1006	I1007	I1008	I1009	I101	I1010	I1011	I1012	I1013	I1014	I1015	I1016	I101
0	0	1.0	1.0	0.0	0.0	0.0	0.0	0.0	0.0	0.0	0.0	0.0	0.0	0.0	0.0	0.0	0.0	0.0	0.0	0.0	0.0	0.0	0
1	1	0.0	0.0	0.0	0.0	0.0	0.0	0.0	0.0	0.0	0.0	0.0	0.0	0.0	0.0	0.0	0.0	0.0	0.0	0.0	0.0	0.0	0
2	2	0.0	0.0	1.0	1.0	1.0	0.0	0.0	0.0	0.0	1.0	1.0	0.0	0.0	0.0	1.0	0.0	0.0	0.0	0.0	1.0	0.0	0.0	0
3	3	0.0	0.0	1.0	0.0	0.0	0.0	0.0	0.0	0.0	0.0	0.0	0.0	0.0	1.0	0.0	0.0	0.0	0.0	0.0	0.0	0.0	0.0	0
4	4	0.0	0.0	0.0	1.0	0.0	0.0	0.0	0.0	0.0	1.0	0.0	0.0	0.0	1.0	0.0	0.0	0.0	0.0	0.0	0.0	0.0	0.0	0

5 rows × 3726 columns

```
#Creating a dataframe which only includes Sales Items. Customer is
indexed instead.
DfSalesItem = df.drop('Customer', 1)
DfSalesItem.head()
```

	I0	I1	I10	I100	I1000	I1001	I1002	I1003	I1004	I1005	I1006	I1007	I1008	I1009	I101	I1010	I1011	I1012	I101
0	1.0	1.0	0.0	0.0	0.0	0.0	0.0	0.0	0.0	0.0	0.0	0.0	0.0	0.0	0.0	0.0	0.0	0.0	0
1	0.0	0.0	0.0	0.0	0.0	0.0	0.0	0.0	0.0	0.0	0.0	0.0	0.0	0.0	0.0	0.0	0.0	0.0	0
2	0.0	0.0	1.0	1.0	1.0	0.0	0.0	0.0	0.0	1.0	1.0	0.0	0.0	0.0	1.0	0.0	0.0	0.0	0.
3	0.0	0.0	1.0	0.0	0.0	0.0	0.0	0.0	0.0	0.0	0.0	0.0	0.0	0.0	1.0	0.0	0.0	0.0	0.
4	0.0	0.0	0.0	1.0	0.0	0.0	0.0	0.0	0.0	0.0	1.0	0.0	0.0	0.0	1.0	0.0	0.0	0.0	0.

5 rows × 3725 columns

```
#Calculate the Item based recommendation
import numpy as np
# We will normalize dataframe now, due to ..
#I believe we do not need to normalize, but let us compare..
#vectorized
DfSalesItemNorm           =           DfSalesItem           /
np.sqrt(np.square(DfSalesItem).sum(axis=0))
DfSalesItemNorm.head()
```

	I0	I1	I10	I100	I1000	I1001	I1002	I1003	I1004	I1005	I1006	I1007	I1008	I1009	I101	I1010
0	0.333333	0.301511	0.000000	0.000000	0.0	0.0	0.0	0.0	0.0	0.000000	0.000000	0.0	0.0	0.0	0.00000	0.(
1	0.000000	0.000000	0.000000	0.000000	0.0	0.0	0.0	0.0	0.0	0.000000	0.000000	0.0	0.0	0.0	0.00000	0.(
2	0.000000	0.000000	0.408248	0.288675	0.5	0.0	0.0	0.0	0.0	0.333333	0.288675	0.0	0.0	0.0	0.27735	0.(
3	0.000000	0.000000	0.408248	0.000000	0.0	0.0	0.0	0.0	0.0	0.000000	0.000000	0.0	0.0	0.0	0.27735	0.(
4	0.000000	0.000000	0.000000	0.288675	0.0	0.0	0.0	0.0	0.0	0.000000	0.288675	0.0	0.0	0.0	0.27735	0.(

5 rows × 3725 columns

```
# Calculating with Vectors to compute Cosine Similarities
ItemItemSim                                                   =
DfSalesItemNorm.transpose().dot(DfSalesItemNorm)
ItemItemSim.head()

#ItemItemSim.to_excel("ExportItem-Item.xlsx")
# Create a placeholder items for closes neighbours to an item
ItemNeighbours                                                =
```

```
pd.DataFrame(index=ItemItemSim.columns,columns=range(1,10)
)
ItemNeighbours.head()
```

	1	2	3	4	5	6	7	8	9
I0	NaN	NaN	NaN	NaN	NaN	NaN	NaN	NaN	NaN
I1	NaN	NaN	NaN	NaN	NaN	NaN	NaN	NaN	NaN
I10	NaN	NaN	NaN	NaN	NaN	NaN	NaN	NaN	NaN
I100	NaN	NaN	NaN	NaN	NaN	NaN	NaN	NaN	NaN
I1000	NaN	NaN	NaN	NaN	NaN	NaN	NaN	NaN	NaN

```
# Create a placeholder items for closest neighbours to an item
#ItemNeighbours                                                  =
pd.DataFrame(index=ItemItemSim.columns,columns=range(1,10)
)
# Loop through our similarity data frame and fill in neighbouring
item names
for i in range(0,len(ItemItemSim.columns)):
                                    ItemNeighbours.iloc[i,:9]     =
ItemItemSim.iloc[0:,i].sort_values(ascending=False)[:9].index
    #we only have 9 items, so we can max recommend 9 items (itself
included)
ItemNeighbours.head()
```

	1	2	3	4	5	6	7	8	9
I0	I0	I2	I1	I769	I1134	I705	I704	I1139	I1138
I1	I1	I768	I759	I758	I754	I757	I749	I750	I753
I10	I10	I1699	I1696	I1674	I2102	I19	I1242	I970	I254
I100	I161	I86	I146	I128	I71	I152	I193	I89	I200
I1000	I747	I962	I1041	I893	I930	I1000	I790	I975	I917

```
ItemNeighbours.head().iloc[:11,1:9]
#it needs to start at position 1, because position 0 is itself
```

	2	3	4	5	6	7	8	9
I0	I2	I1	I769	I1134	I705	I704	I1139	I1138
I1	I768	I759	I758	I754	I757	I749	I750	I753
I10	I1699	I1696	I1674	I2102	I19	I1242	I970	I254
I100	I86	I146	I128	I71	I152	I193	I89	I200
I1000	I962	I1041	I893	I930	I1000	I790	I975	I917

ItemNeighbours.to_excel("ExportItem-Item-data_neighbours.xlsx")

Now, we will create a customer-based recommendation for which we need our item similarity matrix. Then, we will look at which items our customers have bought and get the top N neighbors for each item. Afterward, we calculate the customer's purchase history for each neighbor and calculate a similarity score for them. So, in the end, we just have to recommend the items with the highest score.

#Now we will build a Customer based recommendation, which is build upon the item-item similarity matrix, which we have just calculated above.

Create a place holder matrix for similarities, and fill in the customer column

CustItemSimilarity   =
pd.DataFrame(index=df.index,columns=df.columns)
CustItemSimilarity.iloc[:,:1] = df.iloc[:,:1]
CustItemSimilarity.head()

Customer	I0	I1	I10	I100	I1000	I1001	I1002	I1003	I1004	I1005	I1006	I1007	I1008	I1009	I101	I1010	I1011	I1012	I1013	I1014	I101
0	0	NaN	NaN	NaN	NaN	NaN	NaN	NaN	NaN	NaN	NaN	NaN	NaN	NaN	NaN	NaN	NaN	NaN	NaN	NaN	NaN	NaN
1	1	NaN	NaN	NaN	NaN	NaN	NaN	NaN	NaN	NaN	NaN	NaN	NaN	NaN	NaN	NaN	NaN	NaN	NaN	NaN	NaN	NaN
2	2	NaN	NaN	NaN	NaN	NaN	NaN	NaN	NaN	NaN	NaN	NaN	NaN	NaN	NaN	NaN	NaN	NaN	NaN	NaN	NaN	NaN
3	3	NaN	NaN	NaN	NaN	NaN	NaN	NaN	NaN	NaN	NaN	NaN	NaN	NaN	NaN	NaN	NaN	NaN	NaN	NaN	NaN	NaN
4	4	NaN	NaN	NaN	NaN	NaN	NaN	NaN	NaN	NaN	NaN	NaN	NaN	NaN	NaN	NaN	NaN	NaN	NaN	NaN	NaN	NaN

```
# Getting the similarity scores
def getScore(history, similarities):
  return sum(history*similarities)/sum(similarities)
# This takes ages (35 customers * 3725 items)
#We now loop through the rows and columns filling in empty
spaces with similarity scores.
#Note that we score items that the customer has already consumed
as 0, because there is no point recommending it again.
from timeit import default_timer as timer #to see how long the
computation will take
start = timer()
for i in range(0,len(CustItemSimilarity.index)):
  for j in range(1,len(CustItemSimilarity.columns)):
    user = CustItemSimilarity.index[i]
    product = CustItemSimilarity.columns[j]
    if df.loc[i][j] == 1:
      CustItemSimilarity.loc[i][j] = 0
    else:
      ItemTop = ItemNeighbours.loc[product][1:9] #
      #do not use order but sort_values in latest pandas
                                  ItemTopSimilarity    =
ItemItemSim.loc[product].sort_values(ascending=False)[1:9]
        #here we will use the item dataframe, which we generated
during item-item matrix
      CustomerPurchasings = DfSalesItem.loc[user,ItemTop]
                                  CustItemSimilarity.loc[i][j]    =
getScore(CustomerPurchasings,ItemTopSimilarity)
end = timer()
print('\nRuntime: %0.2fs' % (end - start))
#if there occurs a strange error  tz=getattr(series.dtype, 'tz', None) ..
pandas index.. then this might be if you have used int
# as column headers instead of string
  Runtime: 465.06s
```

CustItemSimilarity.head()

Customer	I0	I1		I10	I100	I1000	I1001	I1002		I1003	I1004		I1005		I1006		I1007	I1008	I1009	I101		I1010		I1011		I1012	I1013	I1014		I1015	I1016	I1017
0	0	0	0	0	0	0	0	0		0	0		0		0		0	0	0	0		0		0		0	0	0		0	0	0
1	1	0	0	0	0	0	0	0		0	0.121708		0		0		0	0	0	0		0		0		0	0	0		0	0	0
2	2	0	0	0	0	0	0	0.114834		0	0		0	0.123409	0	0.114834	0.242708	0.242708	0		0	0.247053	0	0		0						
3	3	0	0	0	0	0	0	0		0	0		0	0.128592	0		0	0	0	0		0		0		0	0	0		0	0	0
4	4	0	0	0.122612	0	0	0	0		0	0.365125		0	0.123409	0		0	0	0	0		0		0		0	0	0		0	0	0

5 rows × 3726 columns

#now generate a matrix of customer based recommendations as follows:

Get the top SalesItems

```
CustItemRecommend = pd.DataFrame(index=CustItemSimilarity.index, columns=['Customer','1','2','3','4','5','6']) #Top 1,2..6
CustItemRecommend.head()
```

	Customer	1	2	3	4	5	6
0	NaN	NaN	NaN	NaN	NaN	NaN	NaN
1	NaN	NaN	NaN	NaN	NaN	NaN	NaN
2	NaN	NaN	NaN	NaN	NaN	NaN	NaN
3	NaN	NaN	NaN	NaN	NaN	NaN	NaN

```
CustItemRecommend.iloc[0:,0] = CustItemSimilarity.iloc[:,0]
CustItemRecommend.head()
```

	Customer	1	2	3	4	5	6
0	0	NaN	NaN	NaN	NaN	NaN	NaN
1	1	NaN	NaN	NaN	NaN	NaN	NaN
2	2	NaN	NaN	NaN	NaN	NaN	NaN
3	3	NaN	NaN	NaN	NaN	NaN	NaN
4	4	NaN	NaN	NaN	NaN	NaN	NaN

#Instead of having the matrix filled with similarity scores I want to see the product names.
#Therefore loop:

```
for i in range(0,len(CustItemSimilarity.index)):
    CustItemRecommend.iloc[i,1:] = CustItemSimilarity.iloc[i,:].sort_values(ascending=False).iloc[1:7,].index.transpose()

CustItemRecommend.head()
```

Customer		1	2	3	4	5	6
0	0	I1134	I999	I2128	I2126	I2125	I2124
1	1	I1194	I650	I1133	I1132	I292	I408
2	2	I1165	I168	I169	I272	I299	I394
3	3	I192	I92	I61	I73	I108	I229
4	4	I1165	I280	I1179	I157	I6	I124

CustItemRecommend.to_excel("ExportCustomer-Item-CustItemRecommend.xlsx")

#We have coded a binary recommender engine, which works only sufficient on a smal data set. Let us see in the next chapter if we can enhance the performance and scalability.

2.5.4 A MORE PERFORMANT APPROACH

Using sklearn.metrics.pairwise cosine_similarity

```
import pandas as pd
import numpy as np
#We will use optimized recommender libraries instead of hand
coding the functions like we did in the previous chapter. This
hopefully brings us convenience and performance boost
from sklearn.metrics.pairwise import cosine_similarity
from scipy import sparse
#data= pd.read_excel('/content/gdrive/My Drive/DDDDFolder/
DDDD.xlsx')
def create_DataBinary(data):
  DataBinary = data.copy()
  DataBinary['PurchasedYes'] = 1
  return DataBinary
DataBinary = create_DataBinary(data)
data=DataBinary.drop(['SalesValue','SalesDate','SalesTransactionID'
,'SalesAmount'], axis=1)
DfMatrix    =    pd.pivot_table(data,    values='PurchasedYes',
index='Customer', columns='SalesItem')
DfResetted = DfMatrix.reset_index().rename_axis(None, axis=1)
DfResetted=DfResetted.fillna(0)
data=DfResetted
```

```
data_items = data.drop('Customer', 1)
```
#Starting point now is the same like in our previous approach:

#Compute Item-Item cosine similarity
As a first step we normalize the user vectors to unit vectors.
#Cosine similarity, or the cosine kernel, computes similarity as the normalized dot product of X and Y:
K(X, Y) = X, Y / (||X||*||Y||)
magnitude = sqrt(x2 + y2 + z2 + ...)
```
magnitude = np.sqrt(np.square(data_items).sum(axis=1))
```
unitvector = (x / magnitude, y / magnitude, z / magnitude, ...)
```
data_items = data_items.divide(magnitude, axis='index')
```
#Compute the column-wise cosine similarity using our sparse matrix
```
def GetItemItemSim(data_items):
  data_sparse = sparse.csr_matrix(data_items)
```
#SalesItemCustomerMatrixs=csr_matrix(([1]*len(user_ids), (product_ids, user_ids))) #hier wird das data_items also selbst aufgebaut
#no difference, no matter if you use data_sparse or not?!--> does normalizing make the differnce?
#similarities = cosine_similarity(data_items.transpose())
```
  similarities = cosine_similarity(data_sparse.transpose())#warum
```
transpose?
#similarity=cosine_similarity(SalesItemCustomerMatrixs)#das gleiche, aber ohne transpose-wechselt Zeilen/Spalten
```
  sim = pd.DataFrame(data=similarities, index= data_items.columns, columns= data_items.columns)
```
#Return a Pandas DataFrame Matrix including the Similarities
```
  return sim #why not ,similarities?
data_matrix = GetItemItemSim(data_items)
```
#Compute Customer-Item Matrix to store which SalesItems the Customer has bought.
```
Customer = 0 # The id of the user for whom we want to generate
```
recommendations --> change!
```
CustomerIndex = data[data.Customer == Customer].index.tolist()[0]
```
Get the frame index
```
CustomerItemPurch = data_items.iloc[CustomerIndex]
```

```python
CustomerItemPurch = CustomerItemPurch[CustomerItemPurch
>0].index.values
# Users likes for all items as a sparse vector.
user_rating_vector = data_items.iloc[CustomerIndex]
# Calculate the score.
score =
data_matrix.dot(user_rating_vector).div(data_matrix.sum(axis=1)
)
# Remove the known likes from the recommendation.
score = score.drop(CustomerItemPurch)
#Customer Item Calculation
# Construct a new dataframe with the 10 closest neighbours (most
similar) for each Customer
data_neighbours = pd.DataFrame(index=data_matrix.columns,
columns=range(1,11))
for i in range(0, len(data_matrix.columns)):
                                     data_neighbours.iloc[i,:9]
=     data_matrix.iloc[0:,i].sort_values(ascending=False)[:9].index
#nearest 9 neighbours?
# Construct the neighbourhood from the most similar SalesItems to
the ones the Customer has already liked.
most_similar_to_likes = data_neighbours.iloc[CustomerItemPurch]
similar_list = most_similar_to_likes.values.tolist()
similar_list = list(set([item for sublist in similar_list for item in
sublist]))
#I did just drop nan, but I need to check this since it might result in
wrong recommendations
similar_list = [similar_list for similar_list in similar_list if
str(similar_list) != 'nan']
neighbourhood = data_matrix[similar_list].iloc[similar_list]
# A Customer vector containing only the neighbourhood SalesItems
and the known Customer likes.
user_vector = data_items.iloc[CustomerIndex].iloc[similar_list]
# Calculate the score.
score =
neighbourhood.dot(user_vector).div(neighbourhood.sum(axis=1))
# Drop the known likes.
score = score.drop(CustomerItemPurch)
```

data_matrix

	0	1	2	3	4	5	6	7	8	9	10
0	1.000000	0.705107	0.916830	0.000000	0.001032	0.004268	0.004551	0.003455	0.003455	0.003455	0.002024
1	0.705107	1.000000	0.565765	0.000000	0.005755	0.002243	0.011378	0.001816	0.001816	0.001816	0.002372
2	0.916830	0.565765	1.000000	0.000000	0.001126	0.002088	0.002226	0.001690	0.001690	0.001690	0.002208
3	0.000000	0.000000	0.000000	1.000000	0.932249	0.507131	0.000000	0.000000	0.000000	0.000000	0.000000
4	0.001032	0.005755	0.001126	0.932249	1.000000	0.529529	0.204978	0.172531	0.172531	0.172531	0.095683
...	...	...	...	...	...	...	...	...	...	...	...
3745	0.000000	0.000000	0.000000	0.000000	0.000000	0.000000	0.000000	0.167999	0.167999	0.167999	0.219455
3746	0.000000	0.000000	0.000000	0.000000	0.000000	0.000000	0.000000	0.167999	0.167999	0.167999	0.219455
3747	0.000000	0.000000	0.000000	0.000000	0.000000	0.000000	0.000000	0.167999	0.167999	0.167999	0.219455
3748	0.000000	0.000000	0.000000	0.000000	0.000000	0.000000	0.000000	0.167999	0.167999	0.167999	0.219455
3750	0.000000	0.000000	0.000000	0.000000	0.134852	0.000000	0.266629	0.202452	0.202452	0.202452	0.264461

3725 rows × 3725 columns

Lets get the top 10 similar items for item 0; only works, if items are int, not nvarchar
print (data_matrix.loc[0].nlargest(10))

```
0       1.000000
2       0.916830
1       0.705107
768     0.533081
704     0.442185
769     0.423981
705     0.399591
706     0.397427
1134    0.290744
1135    0.252792
1137    0.220500
Name: 0, dtype: float64
```

JESKOREHBERG

	1	2	3	4	5	6	7	8	9
I0	I0	I2	I1	I769	I1137	I1135	I1134	I704	I1139
I1	I1	I768	I759	I758	I754	I757	I749	I750	I753
I2	I2	I0	I1	I769	I1138	I1137	I1134	I1139	I753
I3	I3	I1131	I1177	I1178	I1194	I1126	I1133	I1197	I1196
I4	I4	I379	I246	I382	I381	I280	I380	I650	I64
I5	I5	I2598	I3109	I1906	I3063	I1866	I2292	I3399	I3137
I6	I6	I81	I93	I82	I115	I129	I108	I92	I73
I7	I112	I18	I7	I8	I9	I17	I101	I189	I83
I8	I112	I18	I7	I8	I9	I17	I101	I189	I83
I9	I112	I18	I7	I8	I9	I17	I101	I189	I83
I10	I10	I1697	I1672	I2095	I1694	I1242	I19	I254	I1496

2.5.5 CODE BETTER

Let's now see if we can further improve the recommending code.

```python
import pandas as pd
import numpy as np
from scipy.sparse import coo_matrix, csr_matrix
from sklearn.metrics.pairwise import cosine_similarity
from sklearn.preprocessing import LabelEncoder
from timeit import default_timer as timer


purchase_data=data2


#Compute Item-Item cosine similarity
#Customer list-like, meaning Customer at n-th position of list
purchased n-th SalesItem
#Salesitem also list-like, meaning SalesItem at n-th position of list
purchased by n-th Customer
#Returning an Item-Item Similarity Matrix (array-like)
def GetItemItemSim(user_ids, product_ids):
    SalesItemCustomerMatrixs = csr_matrix(([1]*len(user_ids),
(product_ids, user_ids)))
    similarity = cosine_similarity(SalesItemCustomerMatrixs)
    return similarity, SalesItemCustomerMatrixs


#Compute Top SalesItem recommendations per Customer
#using the Item-Item Similarity Matrix from above cell
#creating a SalesItemCustomerMatrixs which is also an array,
meaning SalesItems per rows and Customer as columns as a binary
incidence matrix
#Top_n can be set by yourself, must be int only
```

```
#Returning recommendations per Customer as a Pandas DataFrame
def     get_recommendations_from_similarity(similarity_matrix,
SalesItemCustomerMatrixs, top_n=10):
                          CustomerSalesItemMatrixs     =
csr_matrix(SalesItemCustomerMatrixs.T)
                          CustomerSalesItemScores     =
CustomerSalesItemMatrixs.dot(similarity_matrix)   # sum   of
similarities to all purchased products
    RecForCust = []
    for user_id in range(CustomerSalesItemScores.shape[0]):
      scores = CustomerSalesItemScores[user_id, :]
                          purchased_items     =
CustomerSalesItemMatrixs.indices[CustomerSalesItemMatrixs.ind
ptr[user_id]:
                    CustomerSalesItemMatrixs.indptr[user_id+1]]
      scores[purchased_items] = -1 # do not recommend already
purchased SalesItem
    top_products_ids = np.argsort(scores)[-top_n:][::-1]
    recommendations = pd.DataFrame(
      top_products_ids.reshape(1, -1),
      index=[user_id],
      columns=['Top%s' % (i+1) for i in range(top_n)])
    RecForCust.append(recommendations)
  return pd.concat(RecForCust)


def get_recommendations(purchase_data):
  # replace Customer and product labels with consecutive integer
ids --> not needed any longer
    user_label_encoder = LabelEncoder()
                          user_ids     =
user_label_encoder.fit_transform(purchase_data.Customer)
    product_label_encoder = LabelEncoder()
                          product_ids     =
product_label_encoder.fit_transform(purchase_data.SalesItem)
  # compute recommendations
          similarity_matrix,    SalesItemCustomerMatrixs     =
GetItemItemSim(user_ids, product_ids)
                          recommendations
```

```
=        get_recommendations_from_similarity(similarity_matrix,
SalesItemCustomerMatrixs)
    # project ids back to original labels
                                        recommendations.index
= user_label_encoder.inverse_transform(recommendations.index)
#wird nur benötigt, wenn man wieder von key auf Klarschrift
zurückmappen will
    for i in range(recommendations.shape[1]):
                            recommendations.iloc[:,   i]   =
product_label_encoder.inverse_transform(recommendations.iloc[:,
i])#wird nur benötigt, wenn man wieder von key auf Klarschrift
zurückmappen will
    return recommendations


start = timer()
recommendations = get_recommendations(purchase_data)
end = timer()
print('\nRuntime: %0.2fs' % (end - start))
```

Compare that result to our attempt earlier: just 0.53 seconds, how fast is that!

```
Runtime: 0.53s

print (recommendations)

    .Top1   Top2    Top3    Top4    Top5    Top6    Top7    Top8    Top9    Top10
0   I769    I253   I1146   I1138   I749    I613    I752    I756    I430    I750
1  I1207    I857   I1706   I2532   I1456   I1120   I1988   I2482   I1888   I1890
2  I1206    I301    I390   I1254   I1453    I15    I1283    I820   I1446    I799
3    I72   I1206    I795    I205    I156    I229    I226    I655    I965    I107
4   I954    I15     I635    I911    I419    I287   I1301    I861    I859    I284
5   I598    I264    I411    I552    I649    I134    I346    I880   I1014   I2676
6    I72    I419    I795    I229    I655    I500    I226   I1206    I514    I911
-   ----    ----    ----    ----    ----    ----    ----    ----    ----    ----
```

```
dfrec = recommendations
dfrec.head()
dfrec.to_excel("ExportCustomerName-Itemname.xlsx")
```

Evaluation: Coverage

```
# calculate the share of items recommended

all_recommended_items = recommendations.values.reshape(-1, 1)
[:, 0]

n_items = len(np.unique(purchase_data.SalesItem))

n_recommended_items = len(np.unique(all_recommended_items))

coverage = n_recommended_items / n_items
print('Coverage: %0.2f' % coverage)
```

```
 Coverage: 0.06
```

```
abs_rec_frequency                =               pd.DataFrame({'recommended':
all_recommended_items,                                                'count':
1}).groupby('recommended').count()

top_5_recs_overall     =     (abs_rec_frequency.sort_values('count',
ascending=False) /

          abs_rec_frequency['count'].sum())[:5]

print('5      most      frequent      recommendations:\n      %s'      %
top_5_recs_overall)
```

```
 5 most frequent recommendations:
                count
 recommended
 I1138          0.025714
 I1146          0.025714
 I1206          0.017143
 I769           0.017143
 I1142          0.017143
```

2.5.6 TURICREATE

Turicreate is an open source ML framework owned by Apple. We can accomplish a long list of ML tasks with it:
https://github.com/apple/turicreate
but we will only pick Turicreate's recommender skills.
Please note, that if you want to run Turicreate on your local Windows 10 machine, that will be a little tricky:
https://pypi.org/project/turicreate/
I recommend to try it out on Colab first, to keep yourself away from suffering right from the start.

```
pip install turicreate

%load_ext autoreload

%autoreload 2

import pandas as pd

import numpy as np

import time

import turicreate as tc

from sklearn.model_selection import train_test_split

import sys

sys.path.append("..")

data = pd.read_excel('/content/gdrive/My Drive/DDDDFolder/DDDD.xlsx')
```

data.head()

```
def create_DataBinary(data):
    DataBinary = data.copy()
    DataBinary['PurchasedYes'] = 1
    return DataBinary


DataBinary = create_DataBinary(data)


DataBinary.head()
```

	SalesDate	SalesValue	SalesAmount	Customer	SalesTransactionID	SalesItem	PurchasedYes
0	2018-09-28	8280.0	10	0	0	0	1
1	2018-09-28	7452.0	10	0	0	0	1
2	2019-04-23	21114.0	30	0	1	0	1
3	2019-04-23	7038.0	10	0	1	1	1
4	2019-04-23	7000.0	2	0	1	2	1

```
def normalize_data(data):
    DfMatrix = pd.pivot_table(data, values='SalesAmount', index='Customer', columns='SalesItem')
    DfMatrixNorm = (DfMatrix-DfMatrix.min())/(DfMatrix.max()-DfMatrix.min())
    d = DfMatrixNorm.reset_index()
    d.index.names = ['scaled_purchase_freq']
    return pd.melt(d, id_vars=['Customer'], value_name='scaled_purchase_freq').dropna()


DataNorm=normalize_data(data)
```

```
print(DataNorm.shape)
```

```
DataNorm.head()
```

```
(12674, 3)
```

	Customer	SalesItem	scaled_purchase_freq
0	0	0	0.377728
9	9	0	0.047214
16	16	0	0.165660
18	18	0	0.037792
22	23	0	0.000000

```
train, test = train_test_split(data2, test_size = .2)
```

```
train_data = tc.SFrame(train)
```

```
test_data = tc.SFrame(test)
```

```
print(train.shape, test.shape)
```

```
# lets try with both dummy table and scaled/normalized purchase
table
```

```
train_DataBinary, test_DataBinary = split_data(DataBinary)
```

```
train_DataNorm, test_DataNorm = split_data(DataNorm)
```

```
DfResetted.head()
```

Customer	0	1	2	3	4	5	6	7	8	9	10
0	0	1.0	1.0	1.0	0.0	0.0	0.0	0.0	0.0	0.0	0.0	0.0
1	1	0.0	0.0	0.0	1.0	1.0	1.0	0.0	0.0	0.0	0.0	0.0
2	2	0.0	0.0	0.0	0.0	1.0	1.0	1.0	1.0	1.0	1.0	1.0
3	3	0.0	0.0	0.0	0.0	0.0	0.0	0.0	1.0	1.0	1.0	1.0
4	4	0.0	0.0	0.0	0.0	1.0	0.0	0.0	1.0	1.0	1.0	0.0

5 rows × 3726 columns

ItemCustMatrixTuri = pd.pivot_table(data, values='SalesAmount', index='SalesItem', columns='Customer')   #SalesAmount vs PurchasedYes, Customer must be int for Turicreate to work, that is why data is used instead of data2

ItemCustMatrixTuri.head()

Customer	0	1	2	3	4	5	6	7
SalesItem								
0	15.611111	NaN	NaN	NaN	NaN	NaN	NaN	NaN
1	8.777778	NaN	NaN	NaN	NaN	NaN	NaN	NaN
2	1.444444	NaN	NaN	NaN	NaN	NaN	NaN	NaN
3	NaN	1.0	NaN	NaN	NaN	NaN	NaN	NaN
4	NaN	1.0	3.473684	NaN	1.444444	NaN	NaN	2.666667

ItemCustMatrixTuri=ItemCustMatrixTuri.fillna(0)

DfItemCustMatrix   = ItemCustMatrixTuri.reset_index().rename_axis(None, axis=1)

DfItemCustMatrix.head()

SalesItem		0	1	2	3	4	5	6
0	0	15.611111	0.0	0.000000	0.0	0.000000	0.0	0.0
1	1	8.777778	0.0	0.000000	0.0	0.000000	0.0	0.0
2	2	1.444444	0.0	0.000000	0.0	0.000000	0.0	0.0
3	3	0.000000	1.0	0.000000	0.0	0.000000	0.0	0.0
4	4	0.000000	1.0	3.473684	0.0	1.444444	0.0	0.0

transactions = pd.read_excel('/content/gdrive/My Drive/DDDDFolder/DDDDCustomer-ItemMatrixImport.xlsx')

transactions.head()

Customer		0	1	2	3	4	5	6	7	8	9	10	11	12
0	0	281	0	0	0	0	0	0	0	0	67	0	0	0
1	1	158	0	0	0	0	0	0	0	0	37	0	0	0
2	2	13	0	0	0	0	0	0	0	0	0	0	0	0
3	3	0	2	0	0	0	0	0	0	0	0	0	0	0
4	4	0	3	66	0	26	0	0	8	2	0	0	0	0

variables to define field names

user_id = 'Customer'

item_id = 'SalesItem'

target = 'PurchasedYes'

users_to_recommend = list(transactions[user_id])

n_rec = 10 # number of items to recommend

n_display = 30

Since turicreate is very accessible library, we can define a model selection function as below

```
def    model(train_data,    name,    user_id,    item_id,    target,
users_to_recommend, n_rec, n_display):

  if name == 'pearson':

      model = tc.item_similarity_recommender.create(train_data,
                                    user_id=user_id,
                                    item_id=item_id,
                                    target=target,
                              similarity_type='pearson')

  elif name == 'cosine':

      model = tc.item_similarity_recommender.create(train_data,
                                    user_id=user_id,
                                    item_id=item_id,
                                    target=target,
                              similarity_type='cosine')
```

#Pearson Correlation is simply centered cosine similarity. Pearson correlation is usually used if ratings are in common scaling.

```
      recom   =   model.recommend(users=users_to_recommend,
k=n_rec)

  recom.print_rows(n_display)

  return model


customers=DfCustomerUnique

customers.head()
```

```
     Customer

0         0

1         1

2         2

3         3

4         4
```

variables to define field names

user_id = 'Customer'

item_id = 'SalesItem'

users_to_recommend = list(customers[user_id])

n_rec = 10 # number of items to recommend

n_display = 30

train.groupby(by=item_id)
['PurchasedYes'].sum().sort_values(ascending=False).head(20)

```
SalesItem
I20      2380
I104     2110
I110     1863
I103     1801
I83      1640
I67      1596
I120     1471
I229     1435
I108     1394
I92      1319
I91      1257
I101     1198
I514     1179
I63      1132
I165     1111
I122     1095
I156     1060
I161     1055
I66      1028
I105      998
Name: PurchasedYes, dtype: int64
```

name = 'cosine'

target = 'PurchasedYes'

cos = model(train_data, name, user_id, item_id, target, users_to_recommend, n_rec, n_display)

```
Preparing data set.
    Data has 273137 observations with 35 users and 3663 items.
    Data prepared in: 0.216968s
Training model from provided data.
Gathering per-item and per-user statistics.
+-----------------------------------+------------+
| Elapsed Time (Item Statistics) | % Complete |
+-----------------------------------+------------+
| 967us                             | 100        |
+-----------------------------------+------------+
Setting up lookup tables.
Processing data in one pass using dense lookup tables.
+----------------------------------------+-----------------+-----------------+
| Elapsed Time (Constructing Lookups) | Total % Complete | Items Processed |
+----------------------------------------+-----------------+-----------------+
| 10.223ms                               | 44.75           | 1639            |
| 354.024ms                              | 100             | 3663            |
+----------------------------------------+-----------------+-----------------+
Finalizing lookup tables.
Generating candidate set for working with new users.
Finished training in 1.38358s

+----------+-----------+------------------------+------+
| Customer | SalesItem |         score          | rank |
+----------+-----------+------------------------+------+
|     0    |    I753   |   0.6333644787470499   |   1  |
|     0    |    I758   |   0.624368409315745    |   2  |
|     0    |    I757   |   0.624368409315745    |   3  |
|     0    |    I430   |   0.5863815546035767   |   4  |
|     0    |   I1137   |   0.5847456256548563   |   5  |
|     0    |   I1138   |   0.5847456256548563   |   6  |
|     0    |   I1139   |   0.5847456256548563   |   7  |
|     0    |    I769   |   0.5847456256548563   |   8  |
|     0    |    I749   |   0.5840431650479635   |   9  |
|     0    |    I754   |   0.5840431650479635   |  10  |
|     1    |   I1612   |   0.21305563973217476  |   1  |
|     1    |   I1588   |   0.21305563973217476  |   2  |
|     1    |   I1551   |   0.206958078756565    |   3  |
|     1    |   I1686   |   0.206958078756565    |   4  |
|     1    |   I1764   |   0.206958078756565    |   5  |
|     1    |   I1610   |   0.206958078756565    |   6  |
|     1    |   I1655   |   0.206958078756565    |   7  |
|     1    |   I1609   |   0.206958078756565    |   8  |
|     1    |   I1618   |   0.206958078756565    |   9  |
|     1    |   I1772   |   0.206958078756565    |  10  |
|     2    |    I206   |   0.04155434184169434  |   1  |
|     2    |    I204   |   0.036345024950199645 |   2  |
|     2    |    I266   |   0.027681106559556645 |   3  |
|     2    |    I966   |   0.025745861765088956 |   4  |
|     2    |   I1356   |   0.024963496578256802 |   5  |
|     2    |   I1407   |   0.02376970184086915  |   6  |
|     2    |    I957   |   0.0237361481293145   |   7  |
|     2    |    I929   |   0.0237361481293145   |   8  |
|     2    |    I299   |   0.023363025009562235 |   9  |
|     2    |    I324   |   0.02204136160865059  |  10  |
+----------+-----------+------------------------+------+
[350 rows x 4 columns]
```

Use the best fitting model:

```
users_to_recommend = list(customers[user_id])
final_model = tc.item_similarity_recommender.create(tc.SFrame(DataBinary),
                    user_id=user_id,
                    item_id=item_id,
              target='PurchasedYes',
              similarity_type='cosine')
recom = final_model.recommend(users=users_to_recommend, k=n_rec)
recom.print_rows(n_display)
```

And finally export the recommendations:

```
df_rec = recom.to_dataframe()
print(df_rec.shape)
CustSelec0 = df_rec[df_rec.Customer == 0]
CustSelec0.head(10)
from google.colab import files
files.download('df_rec.xlsx')
```

2.5.7 TENSORFLOW

Tensorflow Recommenders (TFRS) is a Tensorflow package that was open-sourced by Google in 2020.
Below's code is originally from the Google Brain Team's Github repository:
https://github.com/tensorflow
and has only been amended where necessary for our purpose:

```
!pip install -q tensorflow-recommenders
!pip install -q --upgrade tensorflow-recommenders
```

```
from typing import Dict, Text
import numpy as np
import tensorflow as tf
import tensorflow_recommenders as tfrs
```

```
import pandas as pd
df = pd.read_excel('/content/gdrive/My Drive/DDDDFolder/DDDD.xlsx')
df.head()
```

| | | 51kB 7.8MB/s |
SalesDate	SalesValue	SalesAmount	Customer	SalesTransactionID	SalesItem
0	2018-09-28	8280.0	10	0	0	0
1	2018-09-28	7452.0	10	0	0	0
2	2019-04-23	21114.0	30	0	1	0
3	2019-04-23	7038.0	10	0	1	1
4	2019-04-23	7000.0	2	0	1	2

```
def create_DataBinary(df):
  DataBinary = df.copy()
  DataBinary['SalesAmount'] = 1
  return DataBinary


DataBinary = create_DataBinary(df)
DataBinary.head()
```

	SalesDate	SalesValue	SalesAmount	Customer	SalesTransactionID	SalesItem
0	2018-09-28	8280.0	1	0	0	0
1	2018-09-28	7452.0	1	0	0	0
2	2019-04-23	21114.0	1	0	1	0
3	2019-04-23	7038.0	1	0	1	1
4	2019-04-23	7000.0	1	0	1	2

```
data = DataBinary.drop(columns = ['SalesTransactionID','SalesDate','SalesValue']) #replace df by DataBinary, if only using binary (purchased yes) data for recommending
```

```
data['SalesItem'] = 'I' + data['SalesItem'].astype(str)
data['Customer'] = 'C' + data['Customer'].astype(str)

uniq = data.SalesItem.unique()
uniq = pd.DataFrame(uniq)
uniq.columns = ['SalesItem']
uniq

rat = data[['Customer', 'SalesItem', 'SalesAmount']]

dataset = tf.data.Dataset.from_tensor_slices(dict(data))

ratings = dataset.from_tensor_slices(dict(rat))
SalesItem = dataset.from_tensor_slices(dict(uniq))


ratings = ratings.map(lambda x: {
  'Customer': x['Customer'],
  'SalesItem': x['SalesItem']
})

SalesItem = SalesItem.map(lambda x: x['SalesItem'])
ratings.take(1)
```

```
<TakeDataset shapes: {Customer: (), SalesItem: ()}, types: {Customer: tf.string, SalesItem: tf.string}>
```

#Build vocabularies to convert customer ids and salesitems into integer indices for embedding layers:
```
CustomerID_vocabulary                                =
tf.keras.layers.experimental.preprocessing.StringLookup(mask_to
ken=None)
CustomerID_vocabulary.adapt(ratings.map(lambda        x:
```

```
x['Customer']))

SalesItem_vocabulary                                    =
tf.keras.layers.experimental.preprocessing.StringLookup(mask_to
ken=None)
SalesItem_vocabulary.adapt(SalesItem)

#Define a model
#We can define a TFRS model by inheriting from tfrs.Model and
implementing the compute_loss method:
class SalesItemRecModel(tfrs.Model):

  def __init__(
    self,
    CustomerModel: tf.keras.Model,
    SalesItemModel: tf.keras.Model,
    task: tfrs.tasks.Retrieval):
  super().__init__()

    # Set up Customer and SalesItem representations.
    self.CustomerModel = CustomerModel
    self.SalesItemModel = SalesItemModel

    # Set up a retrieval task.
    self.task = task

      def compute_loss(self, features: Dict[Text, tf.Tensor],
training=False) -> tf.Tensor:
    # Define how the loss is computed.

  CustEmbeddings = self.CustomerModel(features['Customer'])
                          SalesItemEmbeddings              =
self.SalesItemModel(features['SalesItem'])
```

```
    return self.task(CustEmbeddings, SalesItemEmbeddings)


# Define Customer and SalesItem models.
CustomerModel = tf.keras.Sequential([
  CustomerID_vocabulary,
    tf.keras.layers.Embedding(CustomerID_vocabulary.vocab_size(),
64)
])
SalesItemModel = tf.keras.Sequential([
  SalesItem_vocabulary,
  tf.keras.layers.Embedding(SalesItem_vocabulary.vocab_size(), 64)
])

task = tfrs.tasks.Retrieval(metrics=tfrs.metrics.FactorizedTopK(
  SalesItem.batch(128).map(SalesItemModel)
 )
)


# Now we will create the model, train it, and generate predictions:
model = SalesItemRecModel(CustomerModel, SalesItemModel, task)
model.compile(optimizer=tf.keras.optimizers.Adagrad(0.5))

# Train for 3 epochs.
model.fit(ratings.batch(4096), epochs=3)

# Use brute-force search to set up retrieval using the trained
representations.
index                                                         =
tfrs.layers.factorized_top_k.BruteForce(model.CustomerModel)
index.index(SalesItem.batch(100).map(model.SalesItemModel),
```

```
SalesItem)

customers = data.Customer.unique().tolist()
```

```
Epoch 1/3
WARNING:tensorflow:The dtype of the source tensor must be floating (e.g. tf.float32) when calling GradientTape.gradient, got tf.int32
WARNING:tensorflow:Gradients do not exist for variables ['counter:0'] when minimizing the loss.
WARNING:tensorflow:The dtype of the source tensor must be floating (e.g. tf.float32) when calling GradientTape.gradient, got tf.int32
WARNING:tensorflow:Gradients do not exist for variables ['counter:0'] when minimizing the loss.
28/84 [=======>......................] - ETA: 34s - factorized_top_k/top_1_categorical_accuracy: 0.0028 - factorized_top_k/top_5_categorical_accuracy: 0.0087 - factorized_top_k/top_10_categorica
```

Create a df including all recommended items per customer

```
import pandas as pd
fcst = pd.DataFrame()

for x in customers:
  _, SalesItem = index(np.array([x]))
                      fcst            =            pd.concat((fcst,
pd.DataFrame(SalesItem[0, :10].numpy()).transpose()))

fcst['Customer'] = customers
fcst.head()
```

	0	1	2	3	4	5	6	7	8	9	Customer
0	b'I2'	b'I1'	b'I0'	b'I704'	b'I768'	b'I705'	b'I2097'	b'I1408'	b'I2100'	b'I2016'	C0
0	b'I1200'	b'I719'	b'I718'	b'I1199'	b'I1126'	b'I1121'	b'I1209'	b'I2155'	b'I1127'	b'I1781'	C1
0	b'I885'	b'I577'	b'I1043'	b'I1434'	b'I500'	b'I291'	b'I144'	b'I493'	b'I950'	b'I390'	C3
0	b'I1831'	b'I1748'	b'I1745'	b'I1746'	b'I1747'	b'I3111'	b'I2190'	b'I1621'	b'I824'	b'I1019'	C4
0	b'I815'	b'I878'	b'I475'	b'I52'	b'I47'	b'I1105'	b'I967'	b'I1033'	b'I715'	b'I854'	C5

Export the recommended items per customer as an Excel sheet

```
fcst.to_excel('RecFc.xlsx', index=False)
```

2.5.8 LIMITATIONS OF COLLABORATIVE FILTERING

It is the same as we did for our sales prediction. We recommend using past agreements between items and customers to predict future agreements. This already tells us a lot about the Pros and Cons of CF:

CF recommendations use similarities between customers and products simultaneously in an embedding space. Products are more straightforward to compute because they have a smaller set of genres (compared to customers). Therefore product similarity is more meaningful than customer similarity (customers, by nature, have a much broader "variance"). CF systems work well only when there are many more users than items in the catalog and generally enough customer-item interactions (needing serious hardware resources to store the customer-item matrix). Otherwise, it's hard to select groups of customers with familiar tastes: large catalogs with many products that have never been purchased (or just once) don't play well. A highly sparse matrix of interactions makes it challenging to compute similarities between customers and items. As an example, for a customer whose tastes are unusual compared to the rest of the population, there will not be any other customers who are remarkably similar, leading to poor recommendations. CF also doesn't know about context.

In contrast with content-based filtering, which recommends similar items, CF will not recommend them based on feature similarity. If this should be vital, then our solution is going hybrid, meaning combining both methods. If a new customer purchases the first time, there is nothing we can recommend to this customer because we have not yet found any similar customers (cold start, due to no purchase history yet). We must also remember that the recommendations will stay the same as long as no new items/combinations are bought. As a last note, CF can create a rich-get-richer effect for popular items and vice versa for unpopular ones, as well as the overall discussed "bubble effect" (due to similar customer clustering).

EPILOGUE

This book's e-book version will constantly be updated with the current package's development. I hope I could help you on your Python Sales Analysis Journey with this book. It was my pleasure! You are very welcome to get in contact with me anytime: contact@dar-analytics.de

www.ingramcontent.com/pod-product-compliance
Lightning Source LLC
LaVergne TN
LVHW052057060326
832903LV00061B/3097